D1133289

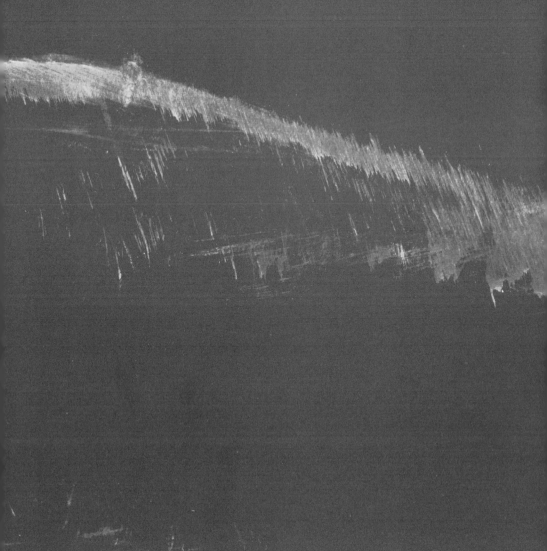

A MODERN DEMONOLOGY

A Modern Demonology

BY

FRANK GETLEIN

ILLUSTRATED BY

ROBERT OSBORN

Being Social Criticism in the Form of a
Scholarly Dissertation, Complete with Sociological Findings Collected by the Latest Approved
Methods, on the Need for a Rehabilitation of
the Ancient Science of Demonology, the
Discovery and Destruction of Demons Inhabiting Various Individuals and Groups
in the Social Order, the Body
Politic and the Economic Milieu.

Clarkson N. Potter, Inc./Publisher
NEW YORK

First Edition October, 1961

Second Edition November, 1961

Library of Congress Catalog Card Number: 61-11427

All Rights Reserved

© 1961 by Frank Getlein
© 1961 by Robert Osborn

Designed by A. Christopher Simon
Manufactured in the United States
of America by
Book Craftsmen Associates, Inc.
New York

*To my father, Frank Getlein, Sr.
and in memory of my mother, Katherine Getlein*

CONTENTS

The Demons

A MODERN DEMONOLOGY

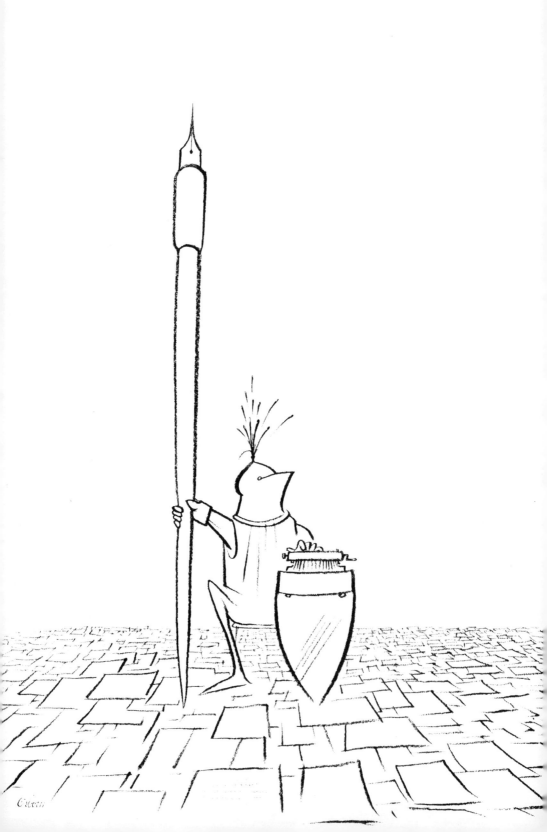

A GENERAL INTRODUCTION
TO THEORETICAL AND
PRACTICAL DEMONOLOGY

THE NEED

𝕴F THE chief purpose of issuing books is to fill a long-felt need —and it is—then a new *Demonology* is centuries overdue. The last notable work in the field was written by King James I of England, who ruled during the first quarter of the seventeenth century.

Our present century—the twentieth—has seen that royal author's other chief work, the *Bible,* replaced time and again. Clearly the companion volume is well due for revision, updating and new packaging all around. With most of today's commerce and industry based securely on planned obsolescence, it is a shame not to take advantage of one of the few authentic examples of natural, unplanned obsolescence still available.

OBJECTION

It may be objected, with a show of reason, that to do so is to call unnecessary and undesirable attention to an article of antique manufacture that has somehow lasted three hundred years and more. Such attention, it may be thought, will inescapably cast aspersion on our own motorcars and washing machines, which, like the may-fly, live for an afternoon and are gone— "shot," as the technical terminology has it.

OVERRULED

The fear is groundless. While the pioneers of obsolescence rarely realize it, most citizens still recall, or at least have heard about, the old days when things wore out by themselves, through use or the passing of time, the days before the ingenious artisan learned to build the end of things into their beginning. The unavoidable reminder, therefore, that King James's book of demons has lasted so long will shock no one.

Its speedy replacement, on the other hand, will remove one possible cause for shock on the part of generations still unborn. And it can—and very shortly will—be easily shown that the good king's work is now utterly obsolete, so much so that it might have been fashioned by a later hand.

The wary should also consider that, in the very nature of things, any demonology compiled today will necessarily have its obsolescence built in, leading to revisions, supplements and new editions at much more edifying intervals than has been the case with the King James version.

A BOON TO SCHOLARS

The revival of the science of demonology will be of the greatest benefit to all parts of the social body. But any such beneficial program for all of society has to begin somewhere and let the benefits spread out from that beginning. The demonological Renaissance, at the dawn of which we stand, will shed its first life-giving rays on the community of American scholarship.

AN OLD CONNECTION

This is entirely fitting and proper, for there is an old connection between scholarship and demonology. The theory and practice of demonology were once the most glowing ornament and useful function of scholarship. There is scarcely a European university of any distinction at all that was not called upon to assist and even initiate the discerning of demons. Here in America, our academic establishment is younger, but even here we once enjoyed the security of knowing our most venerable university to be the intellectual home of our most venerated demonologists. It is so no longer, but it shall be so again.

For if it is true that modern demonology needs all the resources of modern scholarship to explore and codify the rich profusion of material that has grown up like a garden gone to seed since last the job was done, it is even truer that scholarship needs demonology.

THE CRISIS IN EDUCATION

There is a crisis in education. No one any longer attempts to deny this, but there is considerable confusion as to the nature of the crisis. Some say it has arisen from the lack of federal funds being spent on the schools. Some say it has arisen from the threat of federal funds being spent on the schools. Some say it has arisen from the new custom of consolidated schools, with the resulting increase in school busses all on the road at the same time the taxpayers are trying to get to work to earn the money to pay for the schools.

WHAT IS THE TRUTH?

The truth is that all these troubles are merely symptoms, surface manifestations of the true crisis in education. The real crisis is essentially one of overpopulation, the most popular form of crisis today. Needless to say, the academic overpopulation problem is not so much a matter of seats in the kindergarten as it is of chairs in the graduate school.

The truth is we have been brought to the edge of ruin, academically speaking, by our very enthusiasm for learning.

HOW'S THAT?

As follows. The goal of universal literacy in American education was a noble experiment. The trouble arose from the fact that the experiment was a success. Universal literacy has been achieved and the powerful emotional force behind the movement sweeps ever closer to a goal completely unforeseen when the movement started to move, namely, universal graduate studies. Now universal graduate "work," as it is called, is quite different from universal literacy. Universal literacy produced millions of readers capable of reading, among them, everything readable and much that is not, from the racing form and the market report to the most abstract prose of science and the most concrete prose of literature. Universal graduate work knows no such variety. Those who can teach do teach, but what they teach, chiefly, is to teach. In the coming age of the intellect, the great masses of graduate students will learn very little beyond the techniques of being a graduate student, for these are and always have been regarded as ends in themselves.

The proper subject of study is study.

Just so. But the trouble is that the educational wilderness has long been explored, exploited even, the frontier settled, cities erected and moved out of into the suburbs.

AN EXAMPLE

As an example, take literature, a field deceptively accessible because we fancy the materials and the tools to be those we use every day.

A generation ago, the Latin sentences had all been parsed and, Latin being a dead language, no new ones were being brought out. With a conventional show of reluctance, but moved by an absolute inner necessity, American scholarship addressed itself to the English language. After making quite a good thing out of Tennyson and Browning, scholarship, moved by the same necessity, took up the present century. The change broke with tradition but gave honest employment to thousands of scholars who would otherwise have gone hungry to bed.

All the time, however, the scholars in the normal course of their scholarship were reproducing their kind at a far faster rate than poets, or even novelists, could hope to do. The container of literary scholarship swelled far beyond the humble dimensions of the thing contained, the literature.

Scholarship's first response to the new challenge was ingenious but, in the end, self-defeating. This was the manufacture of an entirely new kind of literature, not so much created only to be explicated as created *by* explication. For reasons of speed most of the autoexplicatory literature took the form of poems and short stories, but there were quite a few novels, too. In theory this should have worked. In theory the average alert English department could have devoted half its personnel to writing poems and stories, the other half to explicating them, everybody change at alternate years and time and a half for sabbaticals.

In practice the thing broke down.

What happened was the students caught on to the stratagem. Their first response was to concentrate on courses involving the new literature. This was all to the good. Next, they began writing the new literature themselves, not only graduate students but undergraduates as well. This was mixed. Next they began moving into the faculty themselves, immediately upon graduation and without the customary two or three years in the church schools of the Middle West. This was bad.

There was worse to come.

For the vast majority of the recent graduates joined the faculty, not as lecturers or instructors or laboratory assistants, but as seminar chairmen in creative writing and as writers-in-residence. The latter, in general, are those who have been published outside the quarterlies. Every seminar chairman has, say, twelve students per academic year, each of whom plans to make writing his profession, that is to say, join the faculty. But every writer-in-residence, with no regular roster of students, is a potential influence on every undergraduate in the school. That's how we get to the seating problem. There are just not enough chairs.

More recently, literary scholarship, with the original problem only compounded by the results of explicatory literature, has found another field of operation in the enormous mass of non-literature being published. Literary exegetes have devoted not only individual lectures but entire courses and whole books to such non-literature literature as comic books, daytime television drama, and prose style in advertising. These new preoccupations do not indicate a depraved taste on the part of contemporary exegetes, nor do they imply the decline of the American muse. Rather, they show the sheer desperation of the scholar.

YES, BUT ISN'T IT TIME FOR ANOTHER SUBHEADING?

It is, indeed:

DEMONOLOGY, THE HOPE OF THOUSANDS

Into that scholarly desperation, into the crisis in our educational system, the new and yet old science of demonology will come like a healing balm, like a shaft of light in the darkness, or, to employ the more traditional figure, like a shaft of darkness in the bland and enervating light. Into that revived branch of the higher learning can pour the young scholars in their thousands, assured of getting a job, and assured, much more important, of doing an honest day's work for an honest day's pay, of advancing, be it by ever so little, the edge of the unknown.

HOW ABOUT ANOTHER?

Just a short one.

OTHER BENEFITS

If the most immediate and spectacular effects of the reintroduction of demonology into the curriculum will be the useful employment of thousands of scholars now forced into such academic gray markets as motivation research and public service programming for television, the over-all welfare of the academic disciplines and of the Republic of Letters itself will not be neglected. Far from it.

One of the effects of applying the traditional exegetical methods of literature to non-literature has been a certain blurring of the boundary lines between the various academic disciplines. The literary scholar, for example, who spends a semester investigating the story line in Sexual Aberration Comics can hardly justify his interest in terms of literature. Inevitably he finds himself slopping into sociology and even criminology. Likewise, the savant who takes a grant to analyze the levels of meaning in the televised episodes of *The Kallikak Family* mysteriously finds himself writing economics and even notes on the hard-money problem in a soft epoch.

In justice to the literary scholar, it was not he who began this blurring of the boundary lines. Inspirational medicine began the process with Freud's daring raids into Greek drama and the Russian novel.

But no matter who started it, the flux is on, and the academic benefits of this healthy competition between and within the disciplines are too great to give up. The advent of demonology will intensify this wholesome cross-fertilization in the fields of learning. The nice thing about demonology is that it doesn't really require much specialized training. One can move into it from literature, philosophy, sociology, and, the way things are going, even from the physical sciences.

The new discipline, therefore, can become a scholarly *lingua franca,* the long-sought "core" of the core curriculum, and, not least, an academic territory rather like China before the Boxer Rebellion. With all the Great Powers enjoying trading rights, what jockeying for position can one foresee, what alliances made and broken, sorties attempted, repelled, regrouped, what mad pursuit, what struggle to escape, what pipes and timbrels, what wild ecstasy.

And all the while the Great Powers are struggling to annex the new discipline, the true demonologist will rest secure in the faith that, just as the South came back from crushing defeat to annex the United States Senate, so demonology, by playing world literature against political science, and legislative medicine against advanced fallout, will end up running the show.

STILL MORE

But there is still more.

To some degree—M.F.A., perhaps—the academic benefits outlined above would accrue to the ivy tower from the sudden introduction of any new science open to penetration from all existing departments. One further benefit is demonology's alone to confer. It rises not from the pure but from the applied science of demonology. Just as nuclear physicists were not long content to let Professor Einstein's interesting equation remain a scribble on a blackboard, but felt impelled to grasp this sorry scheme of things and shatter it to bits; just as professors of dramatic expression could not rest while Stanislavsky's dicta were mere program notes, but had to translate them into English and into action, and fill our theaters with mumbles from the heart; just as—well, you have the idea; just so, the revived science of demonology must bring in its train the art of demonology.

From the austere lecture halls the scientists will move into the market place and heap up the fagots. There will be examined, more fully than ever, the stake we have in education. What levels of meaning will be revealed in the old college watchword *Oh, rickety racks!* And in the refrain *The ax, the ax!* Oh then, what mad pursuit, what struggle to escape, what wild ecstasy!

The proper subject of study is study.

Just so. What hitherto-hidden meanings will be found in the physical sciences and in their practitioners when both are studied by the practitioners of the humanities in the light shed by demonology! What unsuspected depths will be revealed in physical education and subsidized football when they are studied demonologically by all the other faculties! What alarming insights will be gained about the liberalism in the liberal arts when the subject is examined impartially, and demonologically, by a fund-raising president and his nervous trustees! Competition is the soul of progress and never more soulful than when the chips are down, fallen where they may, and everyone knows that he is playing for keeps. Demonology stands ready, not merely to meet the crisis in education, but to usher in an era of progress undreamed of heretofore.

The revival of learning is at hand.

A TRANSITION

In reviving demonology as an academic discipline, an effective technique in business and politics, and a new form of entertainment for the entire family, it must be faced that there is much lost ground to be recovered, or, in learned language, much ground to be covered. With the single, rule-proving exception of the War between the States, the history of battles is always written from the point of view of the victor. And this for the best of reasons: there are no historians left on the other side. They were all surreptitiously rooting for the victor all along.

The decline of demonology suffered the common fate. The annals of old England and old New England are full of the triumphs of demonology, but for the period of decline records are few, and those few rather spotty.

We must therefore improvise. The task is to project ourselves imaginatively into the melancholy epoch of the *Untergang* of demonology and find there the reasons for the decline. We can begin no better than with a short eclogue on demonism considered as an adornment of life in the country.

ECLOGUE: DEMONISM CONSIDERED AS AN ADORNMENT OF LIFE IN THE COUNTRY

There is, in America and elsewhere, a whole literature—stories, dramas, poems, novels, songs, and familiar essays, as well as paintings, statues, drawings, prints, photographs, and moving pictures, to say nothing of symphonies, ballets, chorales, oratorios (oratori*i*?), operas, and hoe-downs, and even political platforms, real estate brochures, and outdoor advertising—based on the proposition that the devil lives in town, and that, on its corollary, life in the country is just dandy.

Two explanations suggest themselves. In the natural order the key to this overwhelming testimony may be found in a subtitle of one of the most effective pieces of the testimony. The witness is Beethoven. The piece is the sixth, the "Pastoral." The key title is that of the first movement: "The Awakening of Joyful Feelings upon Arrival in the Country." The conclusion is clear: Beethoven had his joyful feelings awakened precisely because he was *arriving* in the country. He was, essentially, a townsman who came down to the country for a visit and who wouldn't live there if you gave him the place.

In the order of reality, however, the reality that manipulates appearances for its own purposes, it is not unreasonable to assume that the overwhelming testimony about bucolic innocence has been created by the demons themselves as a diversionary tactic.

For the testimony, while unanimous and offered by some of the world's best-loved artists and businessmen, is false.

The apprentice demonologist, on first looking into King James's *Demonology,* receives one overpowering impression: It's so fiendish in the country.

From Pan himself, skipping about in the vine leaves, to the days of good King James, with his tales of cows that won't give milk and demonically managed blights on the crops, the record is clear. When the demons prowl they prowl in the country. Many reasons have been given for the marked preference the demons have historically shown for the bosky. One thinker has it that the demons naturally assail the strongest front of the angelic opposition, the city having long been theirs without a fight. Another attributes to the demons something of Beethoven's joyful feelings: raised in the city, the poor devils rushed off to the country as soon as they could manage it, and, since there is no off-season in demonic activities, the countryside, demonologically speaking, early resembled a kind of Cape Cod without winter.

Invariably such views stem from observers themselves partial to the country, often rural clergymen who have failed to get a living, or receive a call, in a desirable city parish. The truth must be sought elsewhere.

The truth is, of course, that the demons, like the gentle rain from heaven, fall equally upon town and country. The thing is, there's so much going on in town that nobody notices the demons. The farmer works hard, but, at least in King James's day, an awful lot of his work consists in hanging around waiting for nature to get to another stage of the endlessly repeated cycle. The city man may curse the rain, but out he goes in it just the same to get to the next appointment or to the next express. The farmer, waiting for nature to make her move, has the leisure to think about unwelcome rain and thus discern the demons. The town exists for night and entertainment, of every kind and in depth beyond survey. Entertainment in the country? When you've seen one quilting bee, you've seen 'em all.

The main attraction of life in the country is the wealth of idle hours and the luxury of idle minds and idle hands. We all know who finds work for them.

ANOTHER POINT

Malice, too, is a factor in demonism as it is in demonology. The whole field is rife with opportunities to express malice, from the initial pranks with the cows' milk yield to the final drowning of the demon on the ducking stool. Again, the chance for malice has a peculiar attraction in the country. Such opportunities are never rare in town.

THE DEMONS DEPOSED

Once we grasp the essential rusticity of demonism, we see at once why the old gang has fallen on evil days. There isn't any country any more. It's all been subdivided. The very modest requirements of bog and swamp once used for a witches' Sabbath now house a hundred families. There aren't any cattle to inflict with a murrain; and if there were, nobody knows what a murrain is; it's generally thought to be a pile of gravel brought down by the glaciers. Conjure up a storm in the country and the only person you hurt is the greenkeeper. Out in the "real" wilderness, kept that way by stiff zoning ordinances, the landed proprietors are all visitors, really, there by choice, not by need: start any jiggery-pokery with the martini pitcher and they'll just move back to town.

The most telling evidence of the anti-demonological transformation of the countryside into a blighted area where wealth accumulates and men decay is the ritual of ancestral piety known variously as the Brannan Plan, the Benson Plan, the Soil Bank, the A.A.A. and the A.A.A. Plowed Under. There is a covering rationale for all this and even a highly stylized convention of debate about it, but it's pure piety and the biggest breach in the Wall of Separation between Church and State since first we put "In God We Trust" on our coinage.

AN HISTORICAL COMPARISON

In their worst decadence, when they were mixing free love with Greek love and getting freaks, Romans were impelled to maintain, as a propitiatory gesture to past virtue and at considerable expense to the state, the elaborate institution of the vestal virgins, known to later historians as the Lays of Ancient Rome. Similarly, we urban Americans, at appropriately much greater expense, maintain, out of pure nostalgia, an elaborate system we call "Agriculture," though we know very well that the benefited "farmers" are businessmen, like ourselves, who have solved the parking problem and whose bedside reading is not the *Farmers' Almanack* but the *Wall Street Journal*.

Against such an "agriculture" what chance has classical, rustical demonism? None at all. Curdle the milk or frost the crops, crack the earth or spin the cyclone, these latter-day victims have a sovereign remedy against all evil, an exorcism efficacious, a cure that never fails:

More money from the taxpayers.

A KINDLY LIGHT

Amid the encircling gloom one ray of hope appears. More than hope, there is clear promise of the return of demonism in our day, and with it, as day follows night, demonology. This happy circumstance derives from the well-known anthropological phenomenon of cross-cultural influence, which means, among other things, that when one people conquers another the conqueror is to some extent conquered by the vanquished, or vanquished by the conquered—choose one. What happened to the Romans when they rolled over the Greeks has already been mentioned. More recently, in 1066 in fact, the Normans conquered England and became the English. More recently still, only yesterday, it seems, the Americans, in rapid succession, overthrew Mussolini and took up pizza, sank Hitler in the corner bunker and unleashed the Volkswagen, and set the Rising Sun, only to set themselves to writing *haiku* under the bamboo tree.

Inevitably, the same thing is happening in the town-country cross-cultural situation. The farms may have gone urban, what with coaxial television and branch offices of Merrill Lynch, Pierce, Fenner & Smith, but have you seen the city lately? The suburbs alone would amount to a substantial rustification of city life, but there is more to come. Under the auspices of municipal governments, state governments, the Government of the United States and the Downtown Merchants' Association, the American city is moving into Urban Renewal, an organized plan for having grass grow in the streets. The scheme is aimed at the revival of trade. What it will achieve will be the Urbs Garden.

Where you have a garden, you have crops; where crops, a blight; where blight, the demons; where demons, demonology.

23

The chief hopeful sign of the return to rusticity and hence to demonism and thence to demonology, however, is the coming of the age of leisure. If it is true—and it is—that we no longer know a murrain when we see one, it is happily also true that never before have so many people suffered from indolent fever. Once typical of the agricultural scene, that condition, so favorable to the discernment of demons, has now spread through all ranks of society. The age of leisure is with us and we may confidently expect, as in the past, that the devil will find work for idle hands.

The most significant sign of the new age of leisure is the new widespread holding of stocks in corporations. It was formerly thought that demoniacal idleness springs only from manual workers' being limited to forty hours a week, not to mention thirty-five. More recent studies, however, have shown that the man who lives on dividends can be just as idle as the man who works only forty hours a week.

Other researchers have mistakenly concluded that the new idleness is already occupied by such new time consumers as bowling, baseball, Sunday painting, the junior chamber of commerce, television, building an extra room in the attic, motorboating, African violets, barbecues, the Civil War, off-Broadway, SCUBA, Skira, knickknacks on the whatnot, miniature bottles of liquor, full-sized bottles of liquor, the new conservatism, stereophonic sound, and adultery. The fact is that these leisure "activities" are nothing of the sort. They give the illusion of doing something, same as farming in the old days. Like farming, they leave plenty of time for demons.

ANOTHER TRANSITION

There are other good signs for a speedy return of the demons and of demonology, so good in fact that these other signs have actually accomplished that return. It remains only to classify the works of the new demonism and to outline the proper methods of demonology in dealing with demons. Both of these tasks will be begun in the present volume.

The realm of these other signs is political. True demonism, in the old days, carried on its volume business down on the farm, but there was one other important scene of demonological activity. Some of the really choice achievements took place at court.

From this rather unexpected juxtaposition of crown and country, some theorists have assumed a hidden connection between the monarch and the meadow. They cite Mesdames Pompadour and Du Barry and many others, equally at home in the high hall and in the hay. The question is beyond the scope of the present inquiry. It suffices here to know that when the demons weren't at the cows they were at the court.

Courtly demonism always had astonishing versatility, flexibility, and adaptability. You might kill—or, in the language of the day, "make an act of faith" of—any individual demonistic devotee; the demons themselves lived on, often leaping, with breathtaking skill, from demonist deposed to delivering demonologist. This process could move both forward and backward in time. For example, it was fairly common for employed demonologists to discover that the king's cousin, a pretender to the throne, was in league with demons and should be desperately resisted by all the forces of church and state. If, by some fluke, the cousin actually got the throne, the same demonologists were able to discern that actually the late king, and not the cousin, had been in league with demons all the time.

THE DEMONS DEPRIVED

It was this kind of expertise that enabled demonology to thrive for centuries. It was not the loss of the courtly skill in the profession that led to the decline of demonology; it was rather the decline of the courts. The rise of political democracy, such a good thing in many ways, nevertheless led inevitably to the decline of absolute monarchy and thence—unintentionally, perhaps, but nonetheless effectively—to the decline of courtly demonology.

On the face of it, twentieth-century developments have not been heartening. Dr. Gallup has added a new dimension to political

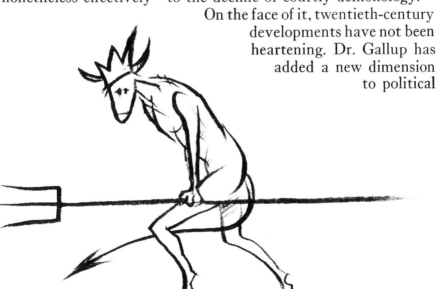

democracy, allowing the country to express its will directly and in advance of events. Motivation research has created consumer democracy, with its root discovery that people *like* to have things fall apart. And so it has gone, with freedom broadening down from precedent to precedent and every step also a step on the heart of the mother science of human culture—demonology.

THE DEMONS REVIVED

Suddenly, at the very heart of the most democratic revolution of them all, demonism and demonology came back to life with a vigor unknown since seventeenth-century Massachusetts. Rasputin, the mad monk of the Romanoffs, had been both demon and demonologist in the court of the czar. It was expected, even by the most loyal scholars, that, when peasants and workers seized the streets of Petrograd, the last bastion of demonism would fall with the last bastion of absolutism.

Nothing of the sort happened. Demonology took on a new lease of life and has been mounting from triumph to triumph ever since. In rapid succession the following demonological battles were fought and won:

The original revolutionists proved that the czar and his whole court were demons, and scattered the lot from the confectionary castles of Vienna and the taxi ranks of Paris to the duplexes of our own Park Avenue. They have never returned.

The bolsheviks unmasked the original revolutionists as demons and scattered *them* from the cellars of the Lubianka to the frozen wastes of Siberia.

The Stalinists discovered that the leader of the Red Army, Trotsky, was a demon and pursued him to Mexico and death by ax.

The new men revealed the old bolsheviks as demons all. The new men also revived the traditional trials and confessions that enrich the seventeenth-century literature in the field. Old demonologists felt a thrill of recognition when the old bolsheviks stood in the dock accused not only as demons but as "mad dogs," a favorite demonic disguise in the old days.

Presently the chief demonologist, Mr. Stalin, was gathered to his fathers and, back on earth, was almost immediately revealed to have been himself a demon, along with the more important new men, most of whom were sent off to jobs in faraway places by the leader of the new new men, Mr. Khrushchev.

This has been demonism in the grand tradition.

Osborn

A DOUBT

Gratifying as all this splendid Soviet work has been, there were from the first serious doubts and reservations among one faction of Western demonologists. With admirably scientific prudence these men pointed out that demonology had been very active in Russia right up to the revolution. What we were witnessing could be simply a cultural lag rather than an authentic revival, a phase in the withering away of the demons.

DISPELLED

Then came Hitler and all doubts vanished. While the Soviet society had turned to demonology in a moment of wisdom as to a rock foundation upon which to build, the National Socialists early proclaimed that the foundation of the new order, the means of building and the goal were all one and the same thing, demonology. There could be no question of folk survivals in the Germany of modern science, Bauhaus architecture, and Alfred Krupp. Here indeed was the authentic new demonology, its legitimacy sealed by the fact that the demons were the Jews, the very people who, in the Golden Age of Demonology, were found always, from Russia to New England, on the side of the demons.

THE NEXT STEP

Almost simultaneously with the brilliant achievements of German scholarship, millions outside Germany were discovering a demonology of their own and discovering the chief demon to be Adolf Hitler. Again, the circumstance had the authentic ring of the classical age. Demonology hadn't given such promise of large-scale political action since the Thirty Years' War.

DANGER

The action came. When it was over, Hitler lay dead in the ruins of Berlin, and there came that moment of universal relief and happiness that always follows success in practical demonology. That very success, of course, was a moment of great danger for the sweet science. To consider two distinct possibilities at that time: Suppose, for example, that the Soviet-American alliance had continued into the time of peace. Or, suppose that the substantial effort the Americans invoked in the cause of war had been turned, unchanged, into the channels of co-operation and enlightenment? Either course could have crippled the revived science in infancy. Both together would have killed demonology in our time.

AVERTED

The moment passed. The destiny that shapes our ends worked busily a day and demonology was preserved. The demons, as they had when Charles the Pudgy lost his kingdom to Black Ludwig, rose from the defeated, hovered in the air a moment, and settled down firmly in the ranks of the Soviet victors.

At the same time, as viewed from the Kremlin, the demons, having hovered, came down unerringly into the hearts and minds of the Western imperialists, or, as they were formerly known, the Democratic Allies in the Great Patriotic War of Liberation of the Motherland.

Thus, unless you happened to be Pandit Nehru—and there aren't many of him—the world was satisfyingly full of demons once more and has remained so to this day. As for Nehru, he has suffered the common and very just fate of those who blind themselves to the demoniacal facts of life: the demons have arrived in unusual numbers: viewed from the East, Nehru is clearly an Imperialist Lackey, not to say Toady; while, from our own point of view, the man is obviously a Fellow-Traveling Dupe of the Commies.

Things have rarely been better.

DEDICATION

All this being so, it becomes the urgent function of scholarship

to gather representative samples of demonic action and demonological recognition, to submit the samples to analysis, and to present samples and analysis, neatly bound, to society, confident that
free men, once they know the truth, will know what to do with it.

To these noble aims, and to good King James, this present
Demonology—only a beginning—is dedicated.

A NOTE ON
METHODOLOGICAL
PROCEDURES

I N THE quest for assurance that both demons and at least a rudimentary demonology still flourish, it was felt desirable and even imperative to set forth from the sheltered halls of learning and actually go to where the demons are found.

Hence our first procedure was to approach the various foundations for assistance in procuring the necessary tools of research, such as transportation money and funds for food and lodging. It is, perhaps, not too surprising that our very modest requests were turned down. Far from being disheartened, we interpreted this finding as confirmation that we were on the right track, that we were indeed building a program far in advance of its time and were but seeing the traditional institutional rejection of the new and significant. The opening of an exhibition of the impressionist paintings of Claude Monet and the occurrence of the annual Columbus Day celebration—both men who pioneered—strengthened our faith.

At this point we had a lucky stroke, one of those break-throughs upon which the advance of learning has always depended. The grandfather of one of our keenest graduate students set up his own foundation. Since we were able to furnish him with documentary evidence that none of the big foundations was remotely interested in our field, he gave us a grant at once.

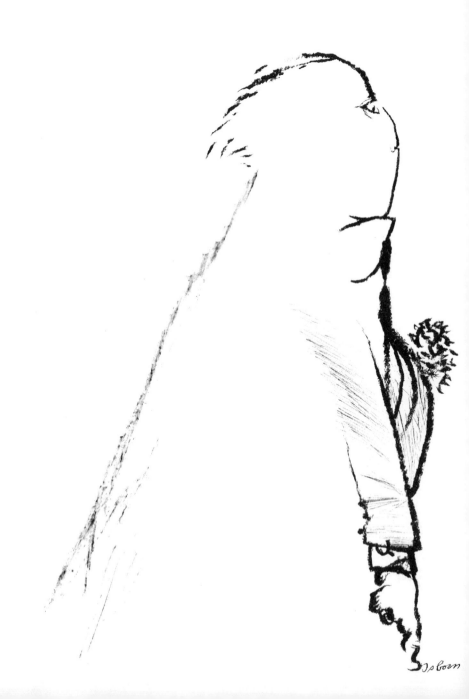

A NOTE ON PROCEDURAL METHODOLOGY

T HE FIRST effect of adequate financing upon the project was a complete overhaul of our techniques. On the basis of years of study, we had prepared a comprehensive demonological questionnaire, we had planned to administer to a representative sampling of the population, securing their co-operation through the presentation of small gifts, specifically ball-point pens for the men and pot-holders for the ladies.

With the grant we were able to adopt more modern methods. With some personal regret but with rigid adherence to the best professional standards, we scrapped the questionnaires and bought a supply of tape recorders in various sizes, equipped with microphones of the highest sensitivity.

Our team of graduate students, after a cram course in electronics, picked up their tape recorders and per-diem allowances and dispersed over the length and breadth of the United States. Wherever possible they gathered their material without the knowledge of the subject, thus avoiding the "sample syndrome" that affects many people when they know they are part of a sociological dip into mass consciousness.

What follows is a selection of the findings. It is presented "raw," with no attempt to edit for unity, coherence, or emphasis or indeed for anything at all except in the case of some of the more colorful profanity. This has been removed in order to allow the book to be sold by mail order, but it has been preserved in our vaults and will be made available on request to any bona fide scholar in this or related fields.

For the benefit of other scholars similarly trapped by technological transition, I pass along the information that we were able, at very slight loss, to dispose of the pens to a used-car dealer and the pot-holders to an aspirant for the U. S. Congress. I am happy to report that we made a small profit on the questionnaires: with almost no changes they were found to be eminently suited for motivation research by a leading maker of motorcars.

The Demons

Osborn

I
DEMONS IN THE
SCHOOLROOM:

NOTE:

THE SUBJECT is the superintendent of schools in the community of Greensward, a prosperous suburb some miles outside a well-known metropolitan area. The place was a local elementary school and the occasion an early fall meeting of the P.T.A. Our graduate student had no difficulty gaining admittance as a young mother. Due to the high sensitivity of the concealed microphone the tape contains a running commentary from certain male members of the audience; this has been eliminated from the transcription.

I

DEMONS IN THE
SCHOOLROOM:

THE CONCEPT of demonism, of course, is an atavistic relic from the dark ages when education was in the hands of ill-prepared schoolmarms in the Middle West and of fanatical, classic-haunted martinets in the East, that is to say, New England, for in those benighted days before John Dewey people hadn't been taught to seek the cause and effect of things and so, rather haphazardly, went about ascribing events and natural phenomena to demons instead of to the actual causes in those cases in which the actual causes were ascertainable and actually that proportion of cases was probably much higher than we think today in looking back on those ages because a good deal of the already-ascertained scientific knowledge had indeed been ascertained—the notion that the earth revolves around the sun rather than vice versa being a reasonably well-known example—but such ascertainable knowledge was withheld from general two-way communication not so much from any active hostility to ascertained scientific knowledge on the part of the educators of those days, who, by the way, are almost always referred to as "teachers" in the surviving contemporary literature of the field, as from the deeply held, fetishistic belief on the part of those educators, or "teachers," that their primary function in the teaching-learning situation was to impart to their students what was smugly known as the "rules" of grammar and syntax and to drill, yes, actually to *drill*, with all the deadly, inhuman repetition that that term implies, to drill those students in what was regarded as the "arts," no less, of how to write an English sentence and how to make it stop.

We have changed all that.

PAST IMPERFECT

It is therefore singularly appropriate that the principal demons menacing American education today are atavars, evolutionary sports, throwbacks to the Middle Ages, survivals of the past, and reactionaries in general. I should like to make the point, parenthetically, that when I use the word "reactionaries," I do so in no political sense whatsoever and I make this point (parenthetically), because when I did use that word I noticed a few of you fathers stir briefly into hostility feelings—an educator has long experience, you know, in seeing what goes on behind the silent faces in front of him—so I assure you that such is not the case, so much so is it not, indeed, the case that let me confide in you that while in principle I believe that every man has a right to his own political convictions, of whatever shade they may be, this principle of mine conflicts with another, even more deeply held principle that, to be effective at all, an educator must sympathize, or "feel with," the community of which he finds himself a part, whose children he hopes to "lead out"—to use the literal meaning of the verb "to educate," from, I believe, the Latin—and therefore I feel no hesitation in telling you that although when I was at the Educational Institute I cast my first ballot for the Progressive ticket of Mr. Wallace, that being the climate of opinion at the Institute at that time, since receiving the call to Greensward I have unhesitatingly joined my new neighbors in going down the line for Ike and Dick and, more recently, for Dick and Cabot.

NOMINATIVE

By the way I know that some of you fathers and mothers are active politically—I certainly received telephone calls from many of you during last year's festivities—and if any of you know whatever happened to the "Henry" in Henry Cabot Lodge I'd appreciate hearing it after the meeting. I may as well tell you I have two reasons for that, one of which is a detached, scholarly interest in the changes that occur to words and the other of which is my belief that that particular change had something to do with the regrettable results of that particular election. In the first place, I think that when we dropped "Henry" and began speaking only

of "Cabot," it confused people: they weren't sure it was the same man. In the second place, I think it gave people the feeling—completely without foundation in objective fact, I hasten to add—that we had something to hide.

I trust that these unavoidably personal revelations have served the worthy purpose of building rapport between the parents of Greensward and their chief educational administrator. It is a point strongly insisted upon by all modern pedagogical theory that parents and educators have got to work together or they'll be worked separately. You have to watch these children every second.

Do I make myself clear:

Can you hear me in the back?

PRESENT IMPERATIVE

The task before us and by us I mean educators, legislators, parents, and just plain citizens, the task we face is to clear away the last remnants of the past that still survive, like atavars, in our educational system. It's no good blinding ourselves to the fact that those atavars are still around. The work of clearing the ground has begun. It began years ago and I am proud to have played, on the local level, my own small part in the work. You recall that when I came to Greensward the building we are in tonight was known as the "grammar school." What an anachronism! What an atavar, one might say. Well, I am happy to remind you that we now call it, with simple dignity, the elementary, consolidated school. Modest, accurate, and with no distressing overtones of fetish worship.

We have taken another step forward with the beginning of this present academic year and that step is the reason I have decided to address you myself tonight because I know from the reports I get from my associate educators in the classrooms which in turn are based on the reports *they* get from the children themselves that some of you have failed to understand our latest innovation.

Some of you even seem to be hurt by it, to take it as a personal thing and therefore I wish to assure you that such is not the case at all.

GENITIVE

At this time I should like to remind you of an innovation made some years ago and one that has proved to be extremely popular with the young mothers in the neighborhood. That old innovation was the special field trip for the second-grade students on which they were given the experience of mailing a letter. Now I don't mind telling you that when we put that innovation in in the first place we met a certain amount of opposition. One parent, who has since moved to another community, is actually on record, in the minutes of the preparatory meeting with parents for that field trip, as saying the innovation was, and I quote from the record, "A lot of God-damned nonsense."

In all fairness, what kind of two-way communication between the school and the community can we expect if parents are going to take those kind of attitudes?

DATIVE

But and in spite of those discouraging comments, we went ahead and the field trip proved a great success. Parents were notified in advance and every year's field trip saw an increasing number of young mothers on hand to record on film and in motion pictures the experience of little Johnny or Susie as the case may be dropping his or her letter into the mailbox on the corner. Last year, as many of you will recall, Mrs. Rappaport, whose son, Raoul, was discussion chairman of the second grade, recorded the whole experience in color motion pictures with sound and later we all had a very enjoyable meeting watching her films which, at my mediation, became part of the permanent audio-visual archives at the Educational Institute.

It's a very good thing she did, because, after full deliberation, our innovation this year has been to eliminate those experiential field trips to the mailbox.

FUTURE CONDITIONAL

This step has not been taken lightly and I feel you are entitled to a full explanation of the reasoning behind it. There will be time for discussion later.

In making this decision, namely, to eliminate from the second-grade curriculum the traditional experiential field trip to the mail-box, we have been moved chiefly by the consideration that after all we have believed for years that reading and writing are atavars of the past and must be swept aside if any kind of democratic equality is to be achieved in our schools. Both reading and writing, you are aware, are carried on by individuals as individuals; frankly, we only deceive ourselves when we have students or educators read aloud and try to pretend that reading has thusly been made into a group activity. Therefore, with the courage of our own convictions, we ask ourselves, in a group-oriented experiential educational system, what place is there for the atavistic fetish of letter-writing? The answer is clear. And if there is no place for writing letters, there should certainly be no place for mailing letters. We shall not deny to the children that letter-writing is still practiced and if they ask questions about the mailboxes we shall explain what they are simply, without embarrassment, in words they can understand, but we shall certainly not go out of our way to call this survival of an earlier cultural complex to their attention.

ACCUSATIVE

In closing I should like to say a word about the highly organized campaign that has been going on recently and that consists in running down your schools, pretending that the Russians somehow do it better or the English or the French or the private schools or the parochial schools, anyone except the poor, overburdened educators and administrators whose lives of quiet dedication are, I may say, widely unappreciated.

Specific charges made in this deliberate, confidence-shaking whispering campaign will be answered in detail in the ensuing programs of our group in the course of the academic year but right now I should just like to report one interesting item of information.

The sources of the charges have all been classified, distributed, weighed, processed, and analyzed by the giant punch-card computor at the Educational Institute and a median has been established as well as progressive percentiles and a probability curve. All these analytical tools point to just one thing: First, many of the critics of the system send their own children to private schools and hence have no firsthand, experiential knowledge of the subject they discuss so freely. And secondly, every one of the more prominent so-called "critics" without exception gains all or a considerable part of his income in one way or another from writing and furthermore is so situated that the size of his income is directly dependent upon the number of people at any given time who know how to read.

In other words, a pecuniary interest has been established. It's one thing to come to grips with an honest atavar or anachronism, it's quite another to engage in "open debate" with people who are merely fighting for their own selfish ends.

If there are any questions?

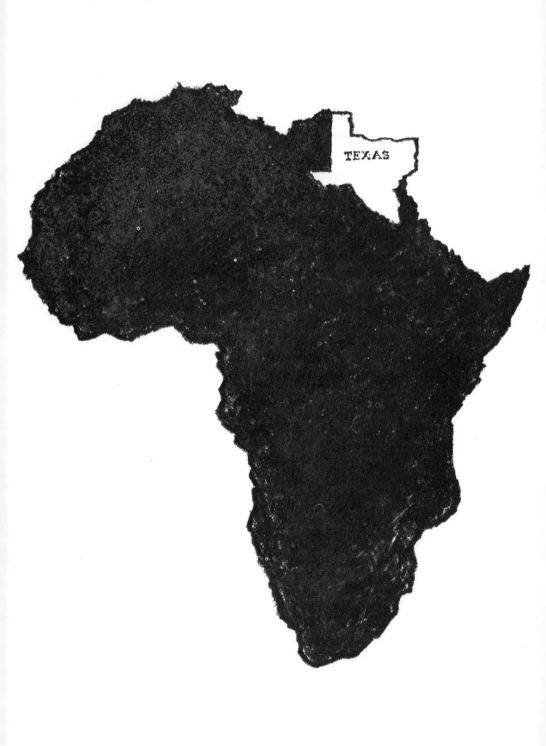

II
THE DEMONS IN
DIXIE

NOTE:

OUR RESEARCH assistant drove out to the manor house of one of the last of the great American plantations and asked the colonel for a statement on a recent Supreme Court decision in the field of education. Actually the original question was never answered, but the assistant on the job was running out of tape and didn't like to ask again.

No suh, Ah wooden lock it if they
was doin' it ta mee but Ahm
diffunt

II
THE DEMONS IN
DIXIE

HE FIRST thing to understand is that nobody, not a person you can find, has a single, solitary thing against the colored people themselves. In their place.

Which is a place made for them by nature and lived in harmoniously for generations. They know their place and they like their place and they only get confused and all stirred up when so-called "reformers" try to move them out of their place and even try to tear the old place down. But in their place you couldn't ask for sweeter people than the coloreds. Gentle folks, who know very well who it is that really has their interests at heart.

And musical. Every one of them can sing. Every one of them's got a voice.

SOUTHERN FRIED

But take them out of their place, or confuse them and get them all stirred up so they leave their place themselves, and they turn into raping, rioting, razoring rascals that you just don't want your children to go to school with.

They take to gin and they take cocaine and they play hot jazz till the cows come home. They wear yellow shoes and they buy black Cadillacs on "easy" payments which are never quite easy enough.

Some of them give themselves airs and become Mohammedans

—though there's nothing wrong with Mohammedans, in their place. Some of them wantonly throw away any airs they ever had and play cool jazz, which is even worse than hot jazz. Hot or cool, you can't get a field-hand chorus to mosey through the gloaming toward the big house, raising those gentle voices in the strains of *I'se Coming, Massa Dan'l, but I Jes' Gotta Rest Awhile* any more. Nobody plucks the old banjo and Stephen Foster's dead. He died, by the way, in drink and despair, brought on by thoughts of things to come. Where did he die? In the North, of course. He died in New York, New York, a well-known town up there.

To lift a gentle darky from the fields of yellow corn, where the order of the rows to hoe but mirrors the profoundly ordered society that grows that corn, and to plunk him down, defenseless, in the jungles of Harlem or of Newport, R.I., is clearly the work of demons. Demons they are, the so-called "reformers" who sweep down like crows upon the corn of an older and mellower way of life.

ROSES FROM THE SOUTH

A few home truths lend themselves to clarifying the shameful story of the demons in Dixie. One is simply that the flower of the Southland is and always has been of Scotch or Scotch-Irish extraction. That being so it becomes highly significant that in the great days of demonology among the seventeenth-century Scots, the king of the demons was always known as "The Black Man."

Further, demonological investigation—conducted by, among others, good King James, himself a loyal Scot who, like so many others, went South—invariably disclosed that the "Black Man" was actually a white man who assumed the ebon hue the better to ruin souls. Now in the demonistic invasion of the South by "reformers" we see exactly the same thing. The leaders and instigators of these unsettling movements are not colored people, but are white people who put on the ebon hue of a pretended interest in the colored lot the better to ruin souls. Many observers find it far from inconceivable that some of those pale-faced "reformers" also, when it serves their purpose, put on the veritable burnt cork to lead "their people" to places they don't really want to go, such as lunch counters and bathing beaches and the front of the bus.

The demons began their work long ago. It is well advanced and solidly entrenched and, it may be, beyond correction now without resort to violence, distressing as that would be to all.

SOUTH OF SCRANTON

They began, the demons, by giving a bad name to slavery. So successfully did they accomplish this, that today it is all but impossible to discuss the subject rationally with those apostles of "tolerance" and "free speech" who have wrought such trouble for the simple of heart. Still, the effort must be made.

Let us begin with the state of the world today. Everybody agrees it's in bad shape and a working majority of the observers agree that a lot of our troubles come from the fact that we are a machine civilization. Everywhere you turn you see the blank face of the machine getting ready to take over. Automobiles run you down. Trains are never on time. Washing machines fall apart and refuse to wash the clothes. In the factories of the North, things are so bad they've got machines to tend machines and other machines to keep the score and reckon the cost.

All this machine mania of ours—from which nine tenths of our trouble comes—is a frenzied search, doomed in the end to frustration, for an artificial, man-made substitute for nature's way of slavery.

It is no longer possible to appeal to man's natural veneration for custom and antiquity and to point out that slavery is an ancient institution, never condemned by any of the world's great religions until fashionable preachers learned to tell their congregations what they wanted to hear. For in today's mad quest for novelty, the very age of an institution is given as the best of reasons for its speedy destruction.

It is no longer possible to appeal to Scripture itself and the comforting story of how the black race began in the sin of one of the sons of Noah. For all that treasury of human experience and divine wisdom is dismissed nowadays as fundamentalist superstition.

SOUTH OF ATHENS

But we may be allowed to point to an ideal age that all accept, the Golden Age of Greece, where all those high-minded pagans strolled in green fields and lolled in the market place, building the epics, dramas, and lyrics, the philosophy and the way of life that have been since then the standard against which man measures his own achievements. It was a lovely age, an age of genius and of gracious living and it was based entirely on the classical institution of slavery. Without slavery the whole crew, from Homer to Euripides, would have had to get off their couch and get a job. There would have been no wily Odysseus at the gates of Troy; he would have been back on the farm, working like a Trojan. The Greeks would have had no more Elgin marbles than they had Elgin watches.

SOUTHERN COMFORT

The only thing the demons took from our common Greek heritage was that regrettable preoccupation with sex that one finds in all the plays and statuary. Consequently the demons have spread it about that resistance to "reform" is rooted in rut, that those who wish to keep their institutions pure are moved by a morbid fear of sexual relations between the races. The whole history of the South—even as that history is simplified in the novels that are this country's *Odyssey* and *Oresteia*—gives the lie to this canard. The Southern gentleman has never willfully denied the pleasure of his company to anyone who sought it and even to some who didn't seek it. Race has been no bar to an evening's entertainment.

That same gentleman, naturally, would rightly point out that, though one brings a well-loved dog into the drawing room to lie before the fire, one does not therefore go oneself to live in the kennel. And that's all the truth there is behind the supposed fear of mongrelization said to guard the purity of the ballot box.

THE MIND OF THE SOUTH

The demons are at work in Dixie and they have powerful allies. But in the end they cannot win; in the end will triumph custom and right reason and the salutary knock on the door at midnight.

The demons propose, with their usual facility, one solution after another for the evils that are of their own making. But their "solutions"—a concession here, a compromise there, a date for compliance and deliberate speed—are vain and valueless. The end of segregation is no solution to anything. Nor, for that matter, is the continuance of segregation. The only solution is the assumption by the responsible elements in the community of the decision-making role required for the welfare of all.

In a word, the return to slavery and the sooner the better.

III
DEMONS IN THE STUDIO

NOTE:

PURE WINDFALL. The material has appeared as the lead article in a certain American art journal three times a year for the last decade. For the sake of form, we read the definitive edition onto tape in the laboratory.

III
DEMONS IN THE STUDIO

T HE PRESENCE of demons in the studios of painters and sculptors will surprise no one familiar with the history of mankind. The studio has been a favorite demoniac haunt, so to speak, from its earliest days. In such primitive societies as still exist, notably in the South Seas and other extension branches of the American Museum of Natural History, it may be observed that the painter-sculptor is wholly employed in demoniac service, using his art to propitiate some demons and cajole others. From this we may argue—on the sound anthropological principle of *Le plus ça change, le plus c'est la même chose*—that in the primitive societies of ten thousand, a hundred thousand, or a million years ago—dealer's choice—conditions were exactly the same.

LINEAR PERSPECTIVE

Moving on to recorded history, we note that in any society of which the righteous were in charge—ancient Israel, Byzantium, Puritan New England—the arts or painting and sculpture were automatically regarded with deep suspicion. The celebrated Golden Calf denounced by Moses was iniquitous not because it was made of gold, as the social realists assert, but because it was made by hand, by an artist. The New England prohibition on playing cards was not primarily against gambling, but against "the Devil's picture book," a phrase of great penetration in linking together the art of painting and the arts of the demons.

Even in this random sampling of the rich history of art as an adjunct of demonism, the observant will have noted that in all cases, from the bison incised in the wall of the cave to the Knave of Hearts doing the dirty in Plymouth and Salem, demonistic art is art that represents the visible world, art that creates an image of man or nature.

Invoking the sound aesthetic principle of *Le plus ça change, le plus c'est la même chose,* we note that this is as true today as ever; in some ways truer, for that old demon, representational art, at last has an adversary, a competitor, a champion of truth, and therefore, as might be expected, the old demon is making extra efforts to crush the truth to earth and to ensure its own survival.

AL PRIMO

As a non-demonistic activity, the art of painting was discovered *circa* 1947 by Jackson Pollock in New York City. For the benefit of older readers, it should be acknowledged that it was formerly thought that painting began with Picasso in Paris in 1906, or with Cézanne in Aix still earlier; these are now known to have been false dawns, heralds, at best, of the savior to come.

The savior arrived on schedule and the new, angelic art of painting reorganized its birthplace so thoroughly that the new work became known as "New York School" painting. Its spread was rapid, chiefly from two early established centers: East Hampton, L.I., where action painting quickly challenged the dominance of adultery as a summertime spectator sport; and in the city of Tokyo, where, just as the early Church Fathers had generously admitted the poet Virgil to be the founder of a kind of pre-Christian Christianity, so the Orientals discovered that all the teachings of Zen Buddhism for centuries had been pointing to the hour of the big drip, a phenomenon, it was noted, dimly prophesied in all those earlier Japanese scroll paintings of waterfalls.

With their customary smiling inscrutability, the Tokyo scholars explained the connection by murmuring the old Zen principle, *Le plus ça change, le plus c'est la même chose.*

JAPONAISERIE

But while Virgil, alas, was not on hand to accept the homage of the Fathers, the New York School received gladly the message of the mysterious East. Studio walls were painted white, floors covered with bamboo mats, feet with sandals isolating the big toe.

The old agnostic faith of the Fathers was given up completely in the rush to Zen, which had a great competitive advantage over Christianity and Judaism in that only the documents were around, with none of the distressing side effects of clerical obscurantism and bourgeois bar-mitzvahs.

The place of sherry at social gatherings was taken by *sake,* the Japanese Sandemann's. That early and authoritative guide to the new art, *Painting Now,* was recalled, revised, and reissued as *Painting Now and Zen.*

The great distinguishing mark of the new painting is its hundred per cent Americanism, a trait that shows in everything from its origins to the enthusiastic abandon with which it is practiced—with which, indeed, it must be practiced.

It is typical of America that simple, plebeian efficiency has given rise to whatever native beauty we have created. The pewter and silver of old New England are cherished as beautiful things, yet they came into existence and took their distinctive forms because the craftsman was in a hurry, because he didn't have too much silver or pewter available, and because his thrifty customers wanted something cheap and serviceable, not something elaborate and expensive.

THE AMERICAN SCENE

So it was with the new painting. The first problem Pollock solved was purely one of efficiency, a problem instantly understandable to the men who made Shaker furniture, or water-powered mills, or the assembly lines of old Detroit. The problem was simply, How to cover the largest possible space of a painting with the least possible expenditure of time and energy?

Stated thus, the problem is one of engineering, and it is as engineers of aesthetic consent that the new painters and their verbalizing champions, or "critics," as they are still called in a lag of language, have made their finest contributions. Pollock solved his engineering problem in a way now famous. Spreading as much canvas as he could get hold of on as big a floor space as he could find, he took cans of greatly thinned paint and dripped it heartily in all directions.

Thus in an afternoon was solved the problem that had baffled every artist in history. The solution was boldly American; it was also authentically American: the emphasis was shifted from the thing made to the process of making, the stress was on efficiency and fast work, and, as other pioneers of production followed Pollock, there ensued a continuing and successful search for new and cheaper materials and methods. Oil paint gave way to automobile enamel, and costly canvas to cardboard sheets.

Most American of all was the astonishing achievement of the new painters in sending their prices to record highs just as their improved methods and cheaper materials were reducing production costs to record lows. Since, with the exception of a reformed dentist or two, none of the new artists has ever been near a business college, this achievement indicates an instinctive grasp of and sympathy for similar feats accomplished in the steel and auto industries.

INDUSTRIAL LANDSCAPE

That sympathy has been returned. If any evidence were needed of the angelism of the new painting as compared with the demonism of the old, it is ready to hand in the total acceptance of the most flashy—and splashy—works by the traditionally conservative pillars of the business community: account executives, public relations men, and network vice-presidents. The true art lover can take pride and hope from the interest in the new painting that has not been forthcoming from businessmen generally since the lush landscapes and even lusher nudes of, respectively, Bierstadt and Bouguereau.

AERIAL PERSPECTIVE

The demons of representational art paint on, refusing to admit that their cause exploded years ago. Their venom against all that is new and exciting is expressed in three ways.

First and worst they have maintained a very firm control over sculpture that the best efforts have so far been useless to break. The basic problem is that sculpture until now has always demanded both relatively hard materials and some minimum of skill; both of these militate strongly against the new spirit. The problem, however, is technical, and will be solved by the appearance on the market of some new, synthetic material with such properties that it could, for instance, be sprinkled in the air, or thrown up toward the ceiling, and yet harden into permanence before hitting the floor and losing that precious shape of the momentary and the accidental.

Secondly, the demons have convinced a number of foreigners that the new painting actually originated in various foreign countries long before 1947 and hence isn't American at all. This is jealous jingoism. In most cases the actual work—not the theory—will be found, as with Mondrian, to be riddled with elements of reason and intellectual control. In those few cases where some apparent resemblance does exist, as in the work of Kandinsky in Munich in 1912, it suffices to point out that this was premature and had no business being done before 1947, by which time Kandinsky was dead.

Third, the demons have on their side most of the leftover critics, who do a great deal of harm, even without meaning to, by applying their old-fashioned methods to the new and exciting work. Nothing can be more fatal to appreciation of an angelist painting of the New York School than a simple description of what it looks like and a reasonable guess as to what materials it is made of.

AUTOMATIC WRITING

Fortunately there is a growing number of verbalizers to expound the inner significances of the new and exciting work. Just as drawing and a familiarity with the properties of oil paint are only obstacles to the practice of the new painting, so an understanding of syntax and grammar is excess baggage that must be got rid of when it comes to art verbalizing. Quickness of mind and a feeling for metaphysical comparisons are the great qualities needed. Thus at an early stage of the new and exciting work, the business community—so traditional, so conservative—showed a certain reluctance to purchase because so many of the paintings seemed to fall apart in such a short time. The verbalizers, ready for all emergencies, discovered on the spot that this quality, very difficult to arrive at, symbolized the times in which we live, was a subtle and poignant reminder of death, and generously ensured, for the first time in the history of art, that the new painting would never become the tyrannical master of future generations—it wouldn't be there to tyrannize.

Authentic verbalization is easily recognized by the high incidence of French phrases and words. *Retardataire* is *de rigueur* when speaking of the old, demonistic art, and *en passant* is always to be favored over "in passing." Partly this is in angry rebellion against the old-style, or *retardataire*, "critics," who always wrote in simple English, thus creating the dangerous illusion that they knew what they were talking about. Partly, French is employed as a gesture of Soviet-American friendship, for this style is really based on that of Dostoyevski's provincial ladies, who never used their own language if they could remember the French of a thing. Mostly, however, French is *comme il faut* as a gesture of cultural piety: even as the Romans, once they'd conquered the world, took up Greek in gratitude to those good old souls who had so added to the pleasures of life, so the new and exciting American art and its loyal verbalizers are glad to recognize the debt we all owe to Paris for the work it did in preparing the world for the coming of the drip.

Even if the true verbalizer has but a single French phrase, he will, for these reasons, use it again and again, varying its meaning as needed, in accordance with his linguistic principle, *Le plus c'est la même chose, le plus ça change.*

IV
AND IN THE MARRIAGE BED

NOTE:

A FAIRLY SIMPLE operation. The researcher, one of our more promising candidates for the degree, early in the project adopted the procedure of carrying his equipment with him at all times. Attending services one Sunday at the church of his choice, he recognized immediately the tone of an authentic sample and threw the switch. Exemplary.

greedles

IV
AND IN THE MARRIAGE BED

God Himself designated the Devil as the Prince of This World. We must therefore never be surprised at the demons turning up any place whatever in the world. All the same it is somewhat shocking to find, in our own century and our own beloved country, the demons making their all-out attack on the sacred institution of holy matrimony itself. After all, the Blessed Mother herself was married. After all, marriage is a sacrament, same as holy orders, though of a lower rank. Some things you'd expect to be sacred, among them the sacraments of the Church. But it was not to be, and we must gird ourselves against the attacks of the demons.

HISTORICAL BACKGROUND

At first they called themselves Birth Control, and they went about peddling their nasty devices to the poor and the down-trodden, the exploited and expropriated, the slum dwellers and wage slaves, decent people, ignorant, to be sure, faithful daughters of the Church mostly but easily seduced by the visiting Protestant ladies with their ribbons and starch, their baskets of cookies and jam, their hints of a job for young Mollie when the girl was ready to enter service.

Did it ever strike you we'd been through all this before? Well, we had then. In the old country they did the same thing and they did it for centuries with no success. They killed the men and they stole the land. When the people were starving, they said, Cry, Down with the Pope. Worship the King of England, they said, and you'll get a bit of soup. Well, we didn't. We held fast and we went without the soup and we wouldn't worship the English king.

We got out of it at last. It was over the sea to the land of the free. But the English had got here first. Not really first, you understand. Christopher Columbus was a Catholic, of course. And before him America was actually discovered by St. Brendan, an Irish priest of God who came over in a coracle. But the English came and stole the land from Columbus and Brendan. So when the rest of us got here, the Protestants were in charge. There was nothing we could do but work on the railroad, dig ditches, and enter domestic service, all at low wages for long hours.

It was into this situation the Birth Controllers moved. Live happily in comfort, they said, by breaking the sacred commands of God. Never mentioning the fact that if their own husbands would pay something like a decent wage, we'd all have been happy in a hurry.

VICTORY AND DECEIT

Well, we beat them back. With our great battle cry, "Not birth control but self-control!" we trounced them so roundly they slunk out of town. Like a thief discovered, they had to change their name. They call themselves Planned Parenthood now and pretend to be several other people. Planned Unparenthood is more like it.

Their siren song today is not about comfort in the slums they built themselves but about the population explosion. The Indians are in danger, they have too many babies. The Indian Indians, not the American Indians. Some time ago the Protestants solved in advance any population explosion among the American Indians. They killed them off and those who were left they locked up in concentration camps. They're still there. You can go and see them. They make pottery and baskets and do rain dances for the tourists. A race despoiled by the earliest form of birth control: murder.

But about the Indian Indians and all their babies. Let's say, for the sake of argument, that the poor Indians are in trouble, they don't have enough to eat. Wouldn't you think that a man with the brains God gave him would say to the Indian, Sit down, friend, and have a bite to eat? Not the Birth Controllers. They say, The reason you're hungry is you're too free and easy in performing the marriage act. Here's a box of our little devices. Just take them along to bed and you'll be all right.

The man is starving!

Or else they say, Just lie down on this table, my good man, while we do this little operation on you. Perfectly painless, fix you up in a jiffy. Co-operate with us and you'll never have to worry about feeding the children because you won't have any children to feed.

I ask you!

MOTIVATION RESEARCH

A point worth noting about India: it used to belong to the English, the Protestants, you know. The Indians finally threw off the British yoke, same as we Americans so long ago, same as we Irish in the grand times of the I.R.A. They're good people, the Indians. The Irish of Asia, you might call them. Our own St. Francis Xavier was out there for years and years, had nothing but praise for them.

Well, anyway, the point I was making. The English ran the country for decades and believe me the Indians didn't get any more to eat under the English than they do under themslves and in all those years there was never a word about the starving Indians or the population explosion. In those days it was hit 'em on the head and grab their jewels and, Oh, the woes of the white man's burden, trudging back to England under the weight of all that loot.

What do you suppose is behind it all, at all?

I'll tell you.

MAJOR PREMISE

It's the same as those Kinseyites a few years back, the godless sociologists from Indiana, a state university, too, I might point out, supported by the taxpayers' money. We can't give a Catholic child a ride to school on the bus at the height of a howling blizzard for fear the Republic would fall, but we can hand over millions to the sociologists to pursue their sexual phantasms.

Well, so. The Kinseyites roamed the country, on the taxpayers' money, and you can bet they didn't eat hamburgers and stay at the Y.M.C.A. While I'm at it, let me tell you about the Y.M.C.A.

Another time.

69

The Kinseyites accosted the women of America with a series of questions fit to be discussed only in the physician's office or the confessional. Naturally, any decent woman slammed the door in their face. The answers, all coming from women who did not mind discussing their intimate lives, were what you might expect, and the Kinseyites issued a famous report that was nothing else but a slander on American womanhood; I don't want to scandalize you, but it was not just fornication and adultery same as any prize-winning novel; all these women "respondents," as they called themselves, from the time they were tots until they were as old as myself, went in for things no honest woman would even know the name of, let alone indulge in.

Without joking, that's what went on in that book.

Osborn

MINOR PREMISE

Now, we ask, why did the Kinseyites do all this? Anyone who isn't blind can see. First they create this picture, this false picture, of the women of America literally going to the dogs and in general behaving like the last days of Pompeii. Now we all know about the carryings-on among the sociologists themselves. They're terrible people, whether in Greenwich Village or Bloomington, Indiana. Wasn't Karl Marx a sociologist? I think he was. So then, when called to account for their behavior, the sociologists turn with a smile of injured innocence, point to their famous report, and murmur in their nice-Nelly way, "Depraved? We sociologists? Why, my dear man, you don't keep up. Everybody does these things nowadays."

Everybody doesn't. Not in any parish of mine, they don't!

CONCLUSION

Anyway, that's the way it is with the Protestant Birth Controllers. They've given up having babies themselves. It spoils their figures, it interferes with their activities, and at the end it's painful and frightening. You all know the old joke about if the men had the babies there wouldn't be any. Well, these women are trying to be men, and, sure enough, no babies.

Not content with that, they itch to have everybody else stop having babies too, so there'll be no difference between them and the rest of the world. The very Hindus put them to shame, so off they go to the Hindus with their devices. But the Hindus are too smart for them. Heathens though they are, they know the natural law and abide by it.

LEX NATURALIS

The natural law is very simple, really. It says bluntly that you have the gift of sex in order to perpetrate the race. The whole thing is a kind of trap of God, actually. When you think of the pain of birth, the expense of raising a child, and the heartbreak they can cause you, who would have children if he didn't have to? The human race would have been out of business years ago. But this is how God outfoxes us. He attaches this great pleasure to the process and people think it's all worth while and the race is perpetrated from generation to generation.

If you try to get the pleasure without the pain, you're a cheat and a thief. When I was a boy we tried stealing apples in the summertime, but it never occurred to us that if the farmer caught us we oughtn't to get a charge of rock salt in the backside. And we did.

It's as simple as that.

If you have some good reason for not having another child—such as the fact that you'll die if you do—your course is clear. All you have to do is practice celibacy. Thousands and thousands of priests and nuns do it all their lives with never a word of complaint. Or, if you want to take a bit of a chance, you can use the Rhythm System.

This has been called "Catholic Birth Control," but it's no such thing. It isn't "Catholic" in any narrow, sectarian way. It's nature's own method, revealed by the wonders of science, though people say the Church is opposed to science. I understand that Birth Controllers themselves use the Rhythm System for that other side of their program they're always bragging about, the so-called fertility clinics.

MAY GOD HAVE MERCY ON US ALL!

Let's take a look at this "population explosion" that's scaring the Protestant Birth Controllers silly. It's going on, all right, make no doubt about that. If, like myself, you had a grammar school to run for the last twenty years you'd know at firsthand that the population explosion is true—though I do think a more dignified name could be found for it.

In the face of such a natural phenomenon of such vast dimensions, the question to ask is, Why? The answer you'll get from the Birth Controllers is all about advances in medicine and fewer infants dead in childbirth and more efficient methods of dealing with cholera and typhoid fever and so on and so on and it's all true as far as it goes, but it really answers the question How? not the question Why?

The reason for this so-called population explosion is crystal clear. Medicine isn't the only field science has been advancing in by leaps and bounds. The most sensational scientific advances in modern times have been made in the ancient art of blowing up your fellow-man. Our future is being shaped by the A-bomb and the H-bomb and I don't know what-all other horrors the wonders of science are discovering this very minute.

Now the Protestants keep telling each other, "Well, with the A-bomb and the H-bomb and the rest, at last we've made war so terrible that mankind will never resort to it again."

Anyone who really believes that just doesn't know mankind. People have been saying that about every new weapon since the slingshot doubled the distance a man could throw a stone at his neighbor.

No doubt the English Protestants said it themselves when they took the rapists and murderers out of British jails and created the Black and Tans. "This army is so fierce no one'll ever fight again." A month later the Black and Tans were over in Dublin massacring our people.

So that's why God has sent the population explosion at just this time. We're on the point of blowing each other up on a scale never before imagined, thanks to the blessings of modern science. When the dust settles—the radioactive dust, at that—what the world is going to need is people, not the "advantages" the Protestants confer on their one-point-four children per family. When the real population explosion comes—namely, the exploding of the population by bombs—the future will belong to those who have reproduced themselves with a good margin to spare.

The future will belong—and, oh, this is the thing that drives those Birth Controllers out of their minds—the future will belong to the Hindus and the Catholics.

GAUDETE IN DOMINO

And I'll tell you something else.

Right now we've got Jesuits, Franciscans, Dominicans, Benedictines, Maryknollers, and all kinds of nuns over there working their hearts out for the conversion of the Hindus.

73

R. OSBORN

V

RUM, ROMANISM, AND REBELLION

$NOTE$:

ONE OF the more difficult, and an excellent example of the value of sufficient funds in scholarly enterprise. The researcher made his way up the Great Valley with pack mule and lived among the residents for some weeks, along the general lines developed by Bronislaw Malinowski during his work in the Trobriand Islands, before gaining access to the ritual at which the following transcription was made.

Osborn

V

RUM, ROMANISM, AND REBELLION

HE PRINCE of Demons is the Pope of Rome. Thousands at his bidding post o'er land and sea, his minions may be found in the velvet-muffled chancelleries of Europe and in the frozen arctic wastes, corrupting the poor Eskimo. His agents are everywhere, and, not least, they are secretly active right here in our own United States. I will deal with the threat to our hallowed freedoms posed by the growing power of Rome in America, Brethern, but first, with your permission and for your enlightenment, I will sketch in brief perspective the role of Rome as the cancer of history. I warn you in advance it will not be a cheering spectacle. There is no cause for optimism when we view the successful perfidy of Rome over the centuries.

As I shall show this morning, dearly beloved, the machinations of Rome have been grinding out their sordid tale of tyranny and intrigue not for hundreds but for thousands of years, while, on the other hand, we here in the Plain Talk Gospel Conventicle have had our corporate existence recognized officially by the sovereign state of California only since the year of Our Lord, nineteen hundred and thirty-one. The papalist myrmidons number in the millions; we are but a handful. The High-rockery of Rome has phalanx after phalanx of ermine-clad cardinals, archbishops, patriarchs, potentates, archimandrites, priests and monsignori, and sisters of all colors and shapes of foreign-looking headdress; here at the Conventicle, Brethern, there's only me, my health is none too good, and when I'm gone I just don't know, humanly speaking, what will be the fate of the Plain Talk Gospel.

When such is the contrast between the contestants, friends, the worldly-wise man may well ask, How do we Conventiclers dare stand up and defy the mighty Church of Rome: I'll tell you Brethern and Sistern, we dare all in spite of the odds, for one simple reason: Rome is wrong, and we are right. They can overwhelm us with force of numbers, they can betray us by treachery, they can put us to the rack, or let us rot in the secret dungeons of the Vatican. Our voice shall not be stilled.

ROME AND A VILLAIN

They call it "Rome Eternal," and they speak truly when they call it so, for hidden in the papalist boast is the ghastly truth. St. John in the Book of Revelations refers to the Pope of Rome as the Scarlet Woman of Babylon. The text is interpreted, outside the Plain Talk Concordance, as meaning the popes are as bad as the rulers of pagan Babylon. Friends, that's only the surface meaning. What St. John is trying, desperately, to tell us there is that the Pope of Rome actually *was* the ruler of Babylon.

And not only of Babylon. When the Children of Israel, the Old Testament forerunners of the Plain Talk Conventiclers, were put down and persecuted in Egypt, I tell you the cruel Pharaoh was nobody else but the Pope of Rome. It's all explained in the Book of Numbers and the explanation is spelled out, verse by verse, in the Plain Talk Concordance. Rome Eternal! Indeed it is. Ah, but the greatest triumph in the long and bloody history of papalism was surely the moment when the popes captured Christianity itself.

Early Christianity, as scholarly investigations have long since established, was actually Protestant. The Catholics didn't come along until much later. In the Acts of the Apostles the Christian Church you read about is quite clearly a Conventicle of Plain Talk Gospelers, with St. Paul of Tarsus filling the job of regional moderator, traveling around from assembly to assembly all over Greece and Asia Minor the same as I do myself through southern California and western Nevada.

PATER PETER

Now, friends, if you ever actually meet a Roman Catholic—and the way the country's going you're more and more likely to every year—he's going to tell you St. Peter was the first Pope. Well, we've already seen how the popes go back long before poor Peter. I guess Cain was the first Pope if there was a first Pope. Or else Lucifer himself. But what about St. Peter? Was he a Pope?

Friends, when you ask the question you answer it. What do we know about St. Peter? He was a fisherman, believed in plain talk, he was a plain man and a Plain Talk Gospel man. He didn't go in for silks and satins and pleasures and palaces. If you talked to St. Peter about the Swiss Guard, he'd probably think you were talking about some gadget you put on a fishing rod to stop back-spin in the reel. No, sir, if poor old St. Peter was a Pope, then the popes have sure changed their way of living and those Roman Catholics will tell you their church never changes. I agree with that; I tell 'em. You got to run on the record, Son, and the record shows that St. Peter just wasn't cut out to be a Pope. Too plain.

THE BIG SWITCH

How it all happened was like this. The popes were actually the Roman emperors. This is all pretty abstruse scholarship and all like that, but the Roman Catholics themselves admit that the Pope's proper title is "Pontifiex Maximus," and this was also the title of the old Roman emperors, the boys that used to lie around swilling wine and burning the Protestants to light their parties or else throwing them to the lions.

Well, about that time the Huns and the Vandals, the Visigoths and Vikings and all that crowd came rolling down to capture Rome because the way the pope-emperors were carrying on was just too much even for those barbarians to stand. The papalists were naturally scared stiff, so in a great hurry they killed all the Protestants and when the Huns entered Rome they cried out that they were just poor Christians and don't hurt 'em.

That's how the papalists captured Christianity. The first thing they did was translate the Gospels into Latin so nobody could understand them and that's how they brought on the Dark Ages. But today, Brethern and Sistern, thanks to Martin Luther we have the Gospel in English and thanks to the Conventicle we have the Concordance and we ought to be grateful because if the popes had had their way, friends, we'd all still be speaking a foreign language to this day.

CONTEMPORARY PROBLEMS IN THE DIALOGUE
OF PLURALISM

Friends, the thing that has made America great is the Wall of Separation between Church and State. All those other countries have gone down, one after the other, because of Roman Catholic machinations. France was a Roman Catholic country and they had the Fall of France in 1940. Italy was a Roman Catholic country and they had Mussolini. Spain is a Roman Catholic country and they've got Generalissimo Francisco Franco. Everywhere you turn the story is the same. But here in America we've got the Wall of Separation to keep the Catholics out and to keep America Protestant.

But, Brethern, there's a breach in the Wall, there's a leak in the dike, the Catholics are pouring in, and we are surrounded by papalists.

Take gambling. Wherever you find a Catholic church, you find Bingo, systematically corrupting the people and breaking down

the habits of thrift and industry that have made America great—along with the Wall itself.

Take drinking. In 1928 we all thought we turned back the Catholic threat. We did, of course, on the surface, but somehow, under the table, the Romanists made a bargain that if they gave Mr. Hoover the Presidency, national prohibition would be repealed. It was and incidentally you can get a good idea of what Catholic promises are worth from what happened to Mr. Hoover.

The great breach, of course, occurred in the election campaign of 1960, when the Democrats, in spite of the clear warning of Al Smith, persisted in nominating another Catholic and when the American people, in spite of the clear warning of Generalissimo Franco, elected that papalist to the highest office in the land.

THE PONTIFF STILL IS SITTING

Now friends, we can see, in the open and without subterfuge, how subtle and Machiavellian the Romanists are. You will recall that during that campaign I gave of myself fully, along with many other dedicated men of God, to warn that the Pope would be in the White House in a month if a certain candidate—and I see no point in giving him free publicity by mentioning his name—were elected. That candidate *was* elected and the Pope still sits in Rome, counting his gold and numbering the Protestants to be killed when the Catholics throw off the mask of tolerance. The Pope still sits in Rome.

Was I, then, a false prophet?

No, my brethren, the Pope still sits in Rome for two reasons. In the first place, he stays there in order to make me out a false prophet and this shows how ingenious and flexible are the minds we have to meet in battle for American freedoms. In the second place, I would not boast, but I am sure the Pope has stayed where he is only because of the effective warning issued by American Protestant preachers, the humble regional moderator of the Conventicle among them, during the campaign.

Therefore, friends, we must not relax our vigilance. Maintain a close watch on the papalist President and scrutinize daily the sailings from *all* Mediterranean ports. As never before, we must make our cry heard, No hope for the Pope!

And while we're about it, it won't hurt to keep an eye on those High-Church Episcopalians.

VI
THE GOSPEL ACCORDING TO
JULIAN THE AGNOSTIC

NOTE:

THIS SAMPLE was recorded at a session of an annual scientific convention. The material, according to the research assistant, although given by an internationally prominent scientist, was given to a poorly attended session scheduled early in the morning after the annual social evening and get-together.

VI

THE GOSPEL ACCORDING TO
JULIAN THE AGNOSTIC

ONE WOULD have hoped—I'm certain Grandfather hoped
—that once mankind had had proved to them that
God is dead, or at least seriously ill, mankind would
have given up its blind allegiance to traditional religion, the era
of peace and plenty and universal brotherhood would have arrived, and we could have seen about using the churches as grana-
ries for bumper harvests that would have resulted.

No such thing happened. Quite the contrary, as is painfully
evident to the delegates in their hotel lobbies and on the streets
of this lovely city, now that God is dead mankind is more devoted
than ever to the musty old religions of the past. We are faced this
morning with two questions:

How has this come about? and

What can we do about it?

INVOCATION

Now I know that some of you are asking yourselves, or even
each other, what on earth or in heaven has all this to do with the
coldly scientific meeting of a body of scientists intent on exchang-
ing information on new developments in biochemistry, biophysics,
and biopolitics. I think I may ask your indulgence and if you but
grant it I assure you the relevance will be clear as I proceed. The
fact is that men of science face a distinct challenge from resurgent
religion. If we do not meet that challenge and face it down, we
must face up to the strong possibility that there will be no bio-

chemistry, no biophysics, not even any biopolitics, but only pious-biology or biopiousity, in either case a new entity with more bias for the pious than the bios.

Gentlemen, when I contemplate this situation and these distinct possibilities, I have the sickening feeling that I've been here before, or, to speak bio-optically, the feeling of *déjà-vu*. The feeling arises from that fact that I have indeed been here before, I have viewed the *déjà*, not only in the person of dear Grandfather, opposed by all those frightful fundamentalists, but earlier still, in those scenes of the very beginnings of science, memories of which are inscribed in the bones and sinews of the halfway-literate man of science if he but knows how to read the inscriptions. I have the chill feeling that I am squatting before a cave and warming my hands at a fire I have myself kindled by rubbing two sticks together, while facing me across the fire is a proto-Presbyterian wearing buffalo skins with the teeth left in. And he chants as they dance, making barely articulated sounds to the effect that fire is a gift of the gods.

BOOM-LAY, BOOM-LAY, BOOM-LAY, BOOM

Flattering, of course, but frustrating, too, to one who would bring light as well as heat to man.

Now we all know the hopes that were raised when Grandfather discovered Charles Darwin. They seemed reasonable at the time and, in the light of the original premises, they still are reasonable. Yet, as the years have passed, religion has, if anything, got stronger, and of course as a result of that wars have gone on, getting worse all the time, man continues to hate his neighbor, and the kingdom of justice is further away than ever.

The reason for this seems to me to be the unexpected and certainly unpredictable flexibility of the organized religions. When we demonstrated beyond doubt that the world had not been made in six twenty-hour days, we had every right to expect that the Pope and the Archbishop of Canterbury would simply slink off the stage of history, overcome with confusion. This to this day they have refused to do. On the contrary, they've joined hands and in an English-Latin interlinear chorus have blandly repeated, "Ah, but look what happened on the seventh day."

They have quoted Freud out of context to infuse new life into the old Garden of Eden myth, and for all I know at this very moment His Holiness and His Grace are concocting some monstrous theogony, using nuclear fission to resurrect the ancient myth of creation, or nuclear fusion to create anew the myth of resurrection.

THE BOOK OF GENESIS

It's enough to make a man doubt the eventual and inevitable triumph of science.

Not really, of course.

Religion and science have a long history together, gentlemen, and well they might, for both came from a single ancestor—magic. I'm as aware as you are that for some years we've been bruiting it about that only religion came from magic and science came from other sources, such as Galileo Galilei, Isaac Newton, Charles Darwin, and my grandfather. As things have turned out, that information was imprecise. The time has come to re-establish the old relationship and get a bit of our own back from the religious demons who for centuries have stolen our thunder to terrify mankind. Science not only is as old as religion, but in instance after instance science has been the victim of religious aggression. The time has come to reverse that relationship. Since the introduction, a few years ago, of the science of religion has had virtually no effect in destroying religious belief, the time has come for a religion of science.

That, too, is older than you might think.

LET US NOW PRAISE FAMOUS MEN

Just to single out a few examples of cryptoscientists corrupted by religion, let us begin with Moses. Again, I know that most of us conventionally regard Moses as a mythic figure, as in the phrase, "the Moses myth," or "the myth of Motheth." That, too, may have been imprecise. Re-examination suggests that Moses was a scientist, and if he was a scientist he was certainly an actual, historical figure: we don't have any other kind in the profession.

We read that Moses was a "sojourner in Egypt," a sojourner apparently being a member of a field expedition. While he was "on sojourn," or in the field, Moses definitely invented bacteriological warfare, a highly sophisticated form of science, and was able to modulate it from crops to livestock to human beings, maintaining, in the final phase, such exquisite scientific control that he was able to single out, for scientific treatment, only the first-born of the several Egyptian families.

Later on, when his obvious gifts had made him an expedition leader, Moses successfully experimented with obtaining water in the desert, a project, I need not remind you, that still kindles the enthusiasm of mankind and the interest of science. It was during that desert expedition that the tragedy occurred. Moses, far in advance of his day in research on meat, was aware that unrefrigerated pork will deteriorate, or "spoil," as the laymen have it, and produce trichinosis. Well, of course, this was centuries before the sheiks of Araby met Standard Oil of New Jersey and there wasn't a refrigerator to be had in all the desert. Determined to save the expedition, Moses went up on a mountain and wrote down a list of sanitary rules for survival under primitive conditions. To get this elementary sanitary code across to his rather simple-minded expedition members, the great scientist, I regret to say, stooped to persiflage and claimed that the sanitary code had been given him by "God," a father-image and symbol of authority that Moses made up on the spot out of his head.

Well, the expedition was saved from trichinosis, but at what a price! As one of those experimental side effects that happen to the best of us, Moses found that he had invented the Jews. The Jews gave rise to the Catholics, the Catholics to the Protestants, the Protestants to the spiritualists, and here we are, up to our acme in religion.

GREGORIAN CANT

Another first-rate scientist was Gregory, better known, I'm sorry to say, as Pope Gregory the Great. Gregory specialized in astronomy and calendar reform and he reformed the calendar very well, although it would be better if New Year's Day were United Nations Day.

Still, there he was in sixth-century Rome and in sixth-century Rome the only way to get anywhere was to be Pope, so Gregory did. Immediately the Church moved in and filled his fine new calendar to overflowing with feast days and fast days, holy days and holidays, saints' days and days for special collections. That's the kind of thing that happens with those people.

WE GO TO DEUT—, WE GO TO DEUT—, WE GO TO DEUTERONOMY

I suggest, gentlemen, that we have taken this kind of treatment quite long enough. I suggest that we strike back. I suggest that we set up a religion of science, in which all men can believe. Appropriate ceremonies can be devised, based on the ritual of conferring the Ph.D. on a candidate. I venture the guess that most of mankind will welcome the bluff common sense of "The square of the hypotenuse equals the sum of the squares of the other two sides," after centuries of the Trinity, predestination, antidisestablishmentarianism, and clerical fascism.

We all know that a new religious venture, to get anywhere at all, needs a strong head, a kind of "pope," you might say, to use the old word, and I know that you people all have your own work piled up in your laboratories. If you care to consider the question I shall be glad to step outside. I shall be in the Masters' Lodge, in fact, awaiting your decision.

Let me offer one final thought. For each of us, wherever we are, let us not curse the obscurantism, let us rather light one little Bunsen burner and show that science, too, can change the world.

VII
DEMONS IN DEFENCE

NOTE:

EARLY IN our program we sent a research assistant to meet and tape a representative of the military establishment in the belief that there, if anywhere, demons are perceived with unusual acuity. The tape was a disappointment. The military representative talked only of his pride in being under civilian control and of the Army's determination to co-operate fully with the Navy and the Air Force in protecting America. As we were going to press, however, the representative turned up at the laboratory as a civilian. He had retired after being passed over for promotion to brigadier. As a service to the pursuit of truth he "leaked" to the laboratory the document reproduced below, which, he said, was lying on his desk at the time of the interview.

Osborn

VII
DEMONS IN DEFENCE

AR-ASN-312-512-46
Classification: *Classified.*
Subject: *Reappearance of demonistic activities in and about*
the Department of Defense.
Object: *These activities shall cease.*

1. THIS DOCUMENT supersedes AR 10/678-543, dated January 1, 1950, titled Appearance of demonistic activities among former military personnel now writing novels. In accordance with instructions contained in the document now superseded, those activities have ceased.

2. It is now clear, however, that the attacks of the demons upon the military establishment of the United States were not centered in the novels of World War II. Indeed, the situation is so grave as to lead some G-2 analysts to suspect that the whole literary tradition of sadistic officers and sexually degenerate enlisted men was merely a feint, a cover for activities of a far more deadly nature. For it is now apparent that, while the novels—and the movies for which they were written—have all vanished from the scene, the Army itself is still around. On the other hand, demonistic manifestations are stronger than ever.

3. It is the opinion of a whole school of top-level intelligence thought that the demonist invasion of the military establishment began with the successful effort to change the name from War Department to Defense Department. "Defense" may have certain values for civilian feelings of righteousness. As far as can be ascertained, consideration for those feelings was uppermost in the

minds of those making the change. Yet, a moment's thought will remind the student of military affairs that, were such consideration to be a factor in military decisions, in all probability armies themselves would have ceased to exist years ago and we'd all be out of a job.

4. From a military point of view, "Defense" has unfortunate connotations of waiting to be attacked, of deliberately assuming the weaker of the two traditional stances. "War Department," on the contrary, very appropriately sums up the great achievement of modern military men. All the ancient fury and devastation are alive in the first monosyllable, while "Department" expresses perfectly the orderly processes by which the Army is conceived, maintained, and deployed.

5. It shall therefore be the duty of all officers of field grade or higher to work whenever possible for a return to the older nomenclature.

GLOOM AT THE TOP

6. The master stroke of the demons to date has been a brilliant attack on the very heart of the military system, command itself. Reference is made to the curious institution known as the "Joint Chiefs of Staff," a contradiction in terms. In successfully placing this revolving committee in charge of all military operations, the demons have paralyzed command and have eliminated the most valuable training ground in command for all levels of field-grade and general officers.

7. As to the paralysis of command: a general officer who finds himself a member of the Joint Chiefs finds also that he is expected suddenly to think in terms of the warfare welfare of the country rather than in terms of the welfare of his own arm. This creates confusion.

8. As to command training: the most secondary second lieutenant knows—or learns quickly—that in military training there is no substitute for actual combat conditions. Close-order drill and cross-country marches are good things, but they are only the foundation upon which true training is built. In a sense, true training is impossible in peacetime, hence the profound regret all feel at the passing of United States military intervention in Latin American affairs. Hence, too, the use of live ammunition in certain training courses: the occasional fatality is not an unfortunate

accident but the thing that gives the training its value and keeps the trainees on the alert.

9. In command, the Army for generations has maintained an elaborate system of combat conditions, in which the officer trainees play, as it were, for keeps. Thus company-grade officers have traditionally sought ways to acquire the maximum of special allowances granted for various forms of special duty. Field-grade officers have competed in enlarging their staffs of personal servants and the amount of military material used in the construction and operation of their domiciles. General officers have competed in evading duty on such large-scale objects as the complete stock of a liquor store in a medium-sized town, and have sought, with even greater success, post-retirement board chairmanships among purveyors of military supplies. Despite occasional lapses of vigilance and resulting embarrassment in the press, the system as a whole has worked admirably. From it have come presidents of great universities and the most imposing array of memoir writers in our time. Truly has it been said, the Battle of Europe was won in the Quartermaster Depot of Fort Benning, Georgia.

10. But the pinnacle and keystone of the entire system were at the top, where dedicated general officers cultivated the friendship of members of Congress, testified voluminously at hearings, and submitted to science-fiction interviews with the press, all with the view of enlarging our own appropriations at the inevitable expense of those of the other branches. Of its nature, the Joint Chiefs concept dislodges the keystone and therefore threatens the entire system of command training.

11. In determining their own degree of co-operation with the Joint Chiefs concept, general officers should be guided by the certain knowledge that, bad as things are, they will become much worse if the Joint Chiefs idea is ever actually made to work.

SCIENCE IN SOLDIERY

12. Destructive as the demonistic deployment described above has been, there are signs that the really massive assault will be launched in the field of military science and in the near future. "Military science," as a technical term, is not used in the traditional sense of keeping the troops baffled, but refers rather to the increasing mutual involvement of the Army and science. There are historians who assert that mutual involvement began with Greek fire—fire being one of the scientific elements to the Greeks

—or with Hannibal's elephants, the science in question being zoology.

13. For the purposes of analysis, it is more useful to assume that the involvement began with the construction and delivery of the crude and primitive atom bomb, which ended World War II.

14. Civilian opinion of that event either deplored the bomb for its immense destruction or hailed it for shortening the war. Both views, typically, missed the point. The real effect of the A-bomb was immediately to deprive some thousands of officers of well-deserved promotions and of the long-envisioned opportunities for advancement and general bettering of one's condition through a major campaign stretched over thousands of miles of sea and land and over months, possibly years. All these dreams went up in the mushroom cloud, and in a few months general officers were scrambling for permanent rank of major. The whole business of nuclear warfare thus began as distasteful and demoralizing. It has not improved.

15. The threat now posed by military science is twofold. One part comes from the scientists themselves—for the most part seized by the Army as legitimate booty of war—who claim that they cannot work without what they call "freedom" and who interpret this freedom to include the right to criticize their military superiors. More long range is the threat that the increasing mechanization of war is going to cut down on the number of general officers needed to staff the computer and calculator units in the decision-making echelons. To this must be added the distinct possibility that the scientific war of the future will be in two phases: the first, all-out science phase will be over in days, perhaps hours, and will be heavily influenced by non-military scientists; the second phase, possibly lasting for years, will be guerrilla, disorganized, local or regional, and probably run by civilians who haven't even been to O.C.S., let alone the Academy

16. A distressing prospect.

SOLDIERING IN SCIENCE

17. Such an attitude, however "justified" by the facts, has won no wars or placed a field marshal's baton in anyone's knapsack. Clausewitz and Japanese wrestlers alike remind us that the consummation of the military art consists in using the enemy's own strength against him. To deal with the long-range threat: when the scientific demons conjure up visions of total destruction, let

us take comfort from our basic superiority: after the destruction is complete, it's going to be a lot easier to reconstruct close-order drill than to do the same for nuclear physics.

18. Furthermore, it is of the essence of the military life that danger breeds opportunity. The dangers of the age of military science are rife with opportunities. For one thing, all this scientific folderol generates widespread feelings that absolute security is vital. This means, if we but keep our heads, that we can go to Congress and demand maximum appropriations while disclosing little or even nothing of what we need the money for.

19. Nuclear explosives and missilery between them are rapidly transforming the upstart Air Force into a kind of artillery. Sooner or later this can be proved beyond doubt even to Congress, and that independent branch can—for purely scientific reasons—be reabsorbed into the Army. It is this kind of imaginative thinking and doing that will win in the age of science.

20. There seems to be little we can do about the Navy in any age.

21. Dismissed.

VIII
'S WONDERFUL

NOTE:

THE SPEAKER was a delegate to the annual convention of the Gentlewoman's League, a national organization of young ladies and young matrons. The researcher reports that the speaker showed an initial reluctance to being taped—possibly this is related to the fear found among some tribes that the camera will capture their "souls" —but graciously acquiesced immediately when she was assured that her remarks would eventually appear in print.

VIII

'S WONDERFUL

THE ARTS in Our Town never amounted to much until the League got behind them. But since that happened, a brief two years ago, the arts have been big time in our neck of the woods as is, I think, adequately witnessed by your inviting me here to explain to League delegates from all over the nation just what it is we have done to the arts in Our Town. I know you didn't invite me for my talents as a public speaker because I just don't have those talents and I suppose I ought to apologize in advance for the lack of what you might call professional polish in my presentation this morning but frankly everything that's happened in the League's Arts for the People Program in Our Town since it began is so wonderful that I haven't the least hesitation in getting up and explaining it all to you in the hope that you can all do something of the same thing for Your Town when you go back home.

It has been a wonderful two years. People have been wonderful. The artists have been wonderful. The newspapers have been wonderful. We all have big scrapbooks which are on the table below me and you are all invited to page through them after my talk. I would say that if it had no other value the Arts for the People Program would be well worth while just for what it's done in calling the attention of the community to the fact that the League exists, that it's a community service organization and is composed of a wonderful bunch of girls. Photogenic, too, as you will see if you accept my invitation to page through the scrapbooks on the table below me after my talk this morning.

Finally, our husbands have been wonderful, just a wonderful

bunch of guys. They've pitched in when they were asked and when they were able to, have supplied us with ever so much material, labor, and transportation and what is in some ways the most precious ingredient of an Arts for the People Program, good will with their business acquaintances in many fields ranging from wholesale groceries to higher education. Most important of all, our wonderful husbands have bravely gone without the pleasure of our company and have learned to do for themselves at home while we were out doing for the Arts in Our Town.

The whole thing began when some of us girls realized that while the League had done wonderful work in medicine and social science and making people aware of political issues facing the nation, it had never done anything for the Muses.

TO CLIO, THE MUSE OF HISTORY

Well, the first job, of course, was to convince the members of the Steering Committee and through them the chapter as a whole. It wasn't easy because an astonishingly high percentage of people, even people educated in the better schools, just don't like the arts. That problem is one that has haunted the Program from its inception and one of our proudest boasts is the way we have solved it on the broad scale, which I'll come to soon. On the narrow scale, that is with our own Steering Committee and membership, we used a more limited but highly effective line of reasoning which you may find useful too.

TO CALLIOPE, THE MUSE OF ELOQUENCE

What we said, simply, was this: The League in our lifetime has been pushed back steadily in one field after another as professionals entered it. Look at the hospitals. The nurses have taken over all the real nursing jobs and all we can do is go around with magazines and candy. Same thing with social service. We don't get to hear these people's problems and help them out any more. The professionals do that. We just drive them to the outpatient ward or the clinic or the divorce court as the professionals tell us. It isn't fair. Why, when my mother was my age, hiring a man to shovel the snow off the carriage drive and the sidewalks was an act of charity and an act of social service. Nowadays we get some mechanized union man to run around in about fifteen minutes with his snowplow and charge plenty for it, too. That's just an example of how private initiative is being killed. The arts are still open, we said, let's get in there while we can.

And that carried the day.

TO TERPSICHORE, THE MUSE OF THE DANCE

The first thing we did was to announce a Fine Arts Ball to raise money for the Program. This got the membership solidly behind us because if there's one thing they like it's a formal dance and if there's a perfect setting for a Fine Arts Ball it's an art museum, which is where we had it. There was some discussion about having a Beaux Arts Ball instead of a Fine Arts Ball, but it was felt that might give people the wrong impression. In your own communities, of course, different conditions may prevail. I'm just describing what we did in Our Town and in Our Town people think the French are immoral anyway and Beaux Arts Ball somehow sounds like people dressing up nude.

I'd like to explain about the finances of the Ball because there has been some misunderstanding about them in Our Town and you may have heard things. The Program netted $6000, roughly, from the Ball. Now it is quite true that we raised $9000 in donations from the Downtown Merchants to pay the expenses of the Ball and because of this there have been some to say that the Program was just a way for the League members to have a good time at public expense. Others say that if we'd just collected the donations and not had the Ball, we'd have been ahead $3000. This is simply not true. Those merchants are donating for Good Will and they want their names in the brochure.

The success of the Ball can best be measured by the sheer space in the newspapers as well as the pictures. That Ball really made the Program known to the people in Our Town and a good time was had by all. Everyone agreed it was the food and the decorations that made it and we simply couldn't have had either and held the price of tickets down to reason for the members if tickets had to carry the whole burden.

TO THALIA, THE MUSE OF COMEDY

From the first moment of actually activating our Program we have had one motto: Art Can Be Fun. We had this printed up in little stickers by the firm that does all the League's printing as their contribution to the program and we stuck the stickers everywhere you can imagine, on lampposts and the back of bus seats, in taxis and powder rooms, on menus and greeting cards. Mary

Lou—she's with me here at the convention—went to the bank and changed all her food, clothing, and household allowance into one-dollar bills, stuck a sticker on every bill and paid for everything with those "marked bills." It would have been interesting to see where the bills turned up, but in a few days all the members were doing the same thing with their allowances, too, and the banks got together and asked our husbands to ask us to stop it. It seems the stickers were not only a hindrance to the machines they have but were probably a criminal offense. I just mention that to show the peak of enthusiasm we reached and have maintained. Oh, it's been wonderful.

But anyway, that wasn't just a motto. When the Program really got going we showed the people that Art really Can Be Fun. We opened our exhibition program with a collection of great cartoons from the *Saturday Evening Post* and the old *Collier's*. We tried to get the artists to contribute their originals, but it's a funny thing we never heard from any of them, so Mary Beth's husband —she's with me at the convention here—had them copied and blown up to large size with some machine he has in his drafting office.

Well, I want to tell you that exhibition drew the biggest crowds the old Cultural Institute had ever seen.

TO EUTERPE, THE MUSE OF LYRIC POETRY

And that's the way we've kept it. People think art is glooming around a musty old museum staring at pictures. It doesn't have to be. Or they think music is Beethoven and Bach and again I say, it doesn't have to be. Our first concert by the Program's symphony orchestra was An Evening with Rodgers and Hammerstein and I want to tell you people who never thought they'd like concert music just loved it. Again, there was some discussion of making the evening one with Rodgers and *Hart* but it was decided that some of Hart's lyrics were just a little fast. It might be all right in the East, which is why I bring it up, but in Our Town Rodgers and Hammerstein are tops. It was wonderful.

A note on getting business support. We hired this wonderful old arranger to weave together a symphony out of the musical themes of television commercials and then got contributions from the local firms or the regional managers in the case of national firms represented in the symphony. This helped very much in defraying the expenses and the symphony itself was the high point of the evening, with everyone on the edge of their seats to see if they could recognize what came next. It was simply wonderful.

TO ERATO, THE MUSE OF EROTIC POETRY

In line with our policy of bearing down heavily on the Fun idea, we decided to make the Fine Arts Ball an annual affair. For the second Ball we had huge signs painted and placed all over town in which *Fine* Arts Ball was repeated right underneath as *Fun* Arts Ball. Again, in using the Ball as the kickoff for the annual drive for public support, we stuck with the stickers only this time, since we figured our slogan was now so well known, thanks to really wonderful coverage from the newspapers, the stickers just said, "It's Fun!" and again they soon appeared in every powder room in town and, I understand, in the best men's rooms as well.

The theme of our second Ball was, appropriately, Art and the idea was for people to come in groups from dinner or cocktail parties and each group, or couples, or even individuals would then pose as a certain work of art. I must tell you the funny remark made by Mary Louise's husband—she's with me at the convention. Jim suggested we all go—well, first of all, I don't suppose most of you know any more about art than we did when we started this wonderful Program so I'd better explain: there's this very famous French painter, David, that's his last name, his first name is Jacques-Louis—no, as a matter of fact it's another French painter, named Poussin, I don't know what his first name is. Anyhow, Poussin has this very famous picture called—well, he was a classical painter and if you remember your Latin, girls, he has this painting about the Romans and the Sabine Women in the early days of Rome. Well, Jim suggested that all the Fine Arts wives go as the Sabines and all the husbands go as the Romans. Jim said that's the only way he could see that they'd ever—well, anyway, it was very funny and of course we all *were* away from home a good deal preparing for the Ball and our husbands have been wonderful about it, just wonderful.

TO POLYMNIA, THE MUSE OF SACRED POETRY

The second Ball, of course, was the time we almost got in *Life* magazine. The photographer came and had lunch with us the day of the Ball, but then he was called away, there was some mine disaster somewhere, but that's just the breaks of the game, anyhow they know about us and sooner or later I think we'll make it.

The great thing about the second Ball was the Art. Most of the artists in Our State are connected with the university and since most of the regents as well as the Republican members of the appropriations committee of the state legislature are related to someone in the League, the university president was very glad to help us out. He got the artists to contribute paintings to the Ball so we had an exhibition as well as the Fine Arts Charades. We also had a competition, with the members of the committee as judges and the painter of the best painting was awarded a free pair of tickets to the Ball. Finally, at the end of the evening, the paintings were auctioned off to the guests, thus raising more money for the Program and getting original art into the homes of the members. All of this activity, of course, made for extra pictures and stories in the papers, so you see how everything goes together in a really well-planned operation.

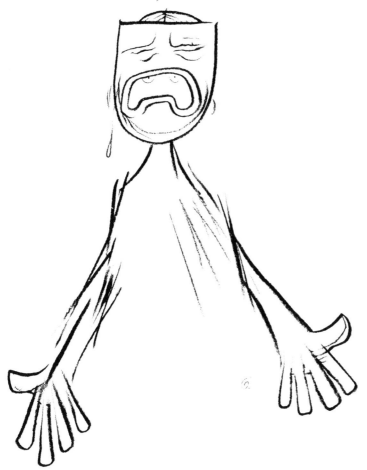

Madam Chairman, in inviting me to speak this morning, asked me to be sure to emphasize the difficulties the Program has encountered and I shall now do that, although I would like to say again that it's just been wonderful, every part of it, and if there have been dark days, they've only inspired us to even greater efforts for the cause of Art.

But there are certain things you have to watch out for, the demons, you might say, that plague such volunteer efforts as ours in Our Town and anywhere else.

One is reporters. Not the newspapers themselves. They've been wonderful. But most reporters, after all, are brought up in a different background and they don't really understand these things. Let me illustrate.

Through some mistake, a reporter from out of town, who had just joined the evening paper, was sent out to cover our Evening with Rodgers and Hammerstein. Well, he just didn't understand at all. He didn't write a word about who was there or comments from the League officers and anything you'd expect. He just wrote his opinion of the whole idea, as though anyone cared what his opinion was. Well, as I say, that was a mistake and the young man left town; I understand he's on some humor magazine now, which, judging from that review, is certainly where he belongs rather than with the Fine Arts.

That's the kind of thing you have to watch for.

TO ORPHEUS, A VERY FAMOUS MUSICIAN

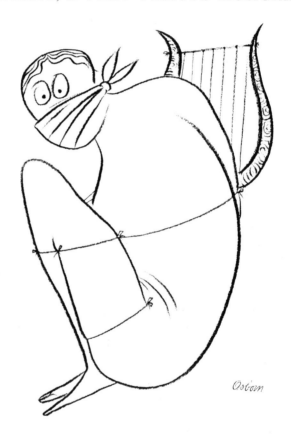

Another thing to watch out for is unions. If your husbands are anything like ours, you already know all about the unions and what frightening power they control, but I have to tell you, girls, that if you want to do anything in the Fine Arts, sooner or later you're going to have to deal with unions, so it's better to be prepared. Again, I shall illustrate.

We made all the arrangements for our second annual symphony concert, An Evening with Irving Berlin, when suddenly, the day before the concert, Mary Jane's daddy asked us to come down to his office. He's the publisher of both the papers in Our Town and he's been just wonderful from the very beginning. Well, Mr. McAllister was in his office and with him was Mr. Paganini, the international representative of the musicians' union. He's a dark little Italian, probably a Sicilian, and he looks like a gangster. Well, Mr. Paganini had the copy for a full-page advertisement he proposed to take in both papers, in which he said that the union was glad to donate its services to the cause of musical appreciation and inviting the public to come, half prices for union members—any union, mind you—which was one of the conditions

we'd agreed to but we expected it to be quietly passed around to any union members really interested in music.

Mr. Paganini said that either the advertisement would have to run or his members would have to be paid, and paid full union scale, too, for the performance. If Mr. McAllister refused to run the ad, Mr. Paganini said he would "pull his boys out" fifteen minutes before curtain time. Well, he had us and we paid but I don't mind telling you it cut down the profits on the concert enormously.

TO ATROPOS, THE THIRD FATE,
THE ONE WITH THE SHEARS

Finally, it is extremely important to keep on good terms with any professionals you have to work with in any of the arts. They're very sensitive, very touchy people and you have to watch everything you say or do, and be very careful to make everything clear to them. For instance, one of the university artists, for his contribution to the second Fun Arts Ball, sent in a simply enormous painting. It must have been ten feet high and thirty feet long and it's just a mess of splashes and roller marks and what not. Very exciting, of course, but so big! Well, naturally, nobody bid on it at the auction—where would you put a thing like that? I was embarrassed and I guess Mary Laurel was, too, because both our husbands began bidding and ran it up to over a hundred dollars. Well, it cost us over fifty dollars to have the thing trucked up to our house. The only place we could get it in out of the weather is the garage which means that all three cars have to sit out in the driveway. And we can't do anything about it because it would offend the artist.

Well, that's what I mean. You have to explain to them about living rooms and things like that.

On the other hand, I must say our relations with our director in the museum have been the best. He left after the second Ball and the Trustees very kindly offered the post to me and of course it saves the museum the amount of his salary because I'm a volunteer. Before he left, our director put all the museum's old pictures away in a vault and he gave me the key in an envelope. "Mary Doll," he told me, "if enthusiasm ever lags and you get in another director from out of town, give him this key, but don't you open that vault yourself, there's nothing there you'd like."

Then he helped me hang my first group of exhibitions that were all my own, although still the Program's, of course. We had the Best Advertisements of local firms in our gallery, the history of the Arts for the People Program in photographs in another gallery and downstairs and along the corridors we had Art by Children of League Members, a permanent but changing exhibition.

When our director left, I realized that the Program had helped his professional career. It must have made him known around the country and made other museums want to get him, because he said, "Mary Doll, if it hadn't been for the League's Arts Program, I probably would have stayed in Our Town all my life." Then he left.

Well, that's about all. All of us here will be glad to meet with any of you after the meeting and I myself will be happy to come out to Your Town to help you get started.

It's been wonderful talking to you, just wonderful.

IX
THE BAD PAD

NOTE:

To secure this unusually rich demonological sample, the researcher let her hair grow quite long, equipped herself with a supply of black stockings and "floated" among the bars of G-------- Village. After a week she sent back the tape here transcribed with a note that she intended to gather more material, a program which we at the laboratory thought superfluous after hearing her tape. She has not been heard of since.

IX
THE BAD PAD

HE DEMONS are teeming in the U. S. of A., Dad. I mean they're like all over the scene. Me, I got a low threshold of tolerance for those screaming demons. Squares from Squaresville don't bug me. They're human, too, or if they're not like human all the way, still they're walking on two legs like everybody else and they got a right. Well, all right, they don't have a *right*, exactly, but there's nothing you can do about it so live and like let live is my slogan, Hogan.

NOTES FROM UNDERGROUND

So it isn't the Squares from Squaresville that throw me into my countdown. It's the Squares from Squaresville that like take it along and bring it down here and try to smother me, Mother, in my own mad pad. I mean, like you can't even take the subway without the Squares cubing it up all over the place. You go uptown you look out the window the sign says, "Grand Central." You know what Grand Central is? It's the local depot where the nine-to-five and still-alive contingent grab the bar on wheels, roll on to Conn., and plant their ass in the grass.

A man can't breathe, man, you got to have air.

So you move to the other side of the tracks and take the downtown tube? Wall Street.

I mean when it comes to cubes these chaps give the old Oh-Ho-Ho to Mies van der Rohe-ho. You got to have air you pay the fare and at the end of the ride where are you? Staten Island, the city of homes.

If you're really serious, man, in the search for your identity, sooner or later you want to rattle on up to Union Theological to hear what Oom Paul Tillich and Big Reinhold have to say. They're like Protestants and all that, but with them it's different. No bean suppers and strawberry festivals. It's all like Sartre and Camus and good old Soren Kierkegaard. Soren himself was a very large Protestant, for that matter, though you'd never know it from Norman St. Vincent de Peale.

I mean with the best will in the world you turn the stile and make the mile for Union and you have to change trains right at the squarest square of them all, Times Square. All that news, man, that's print to give fits, plus the stale, fetid atmosphere of the commercial theater. It isn't the sad vulgarity, it's the squarity. I don't mind the popcorn palaces, the neon nickel-grabbers and the hand-painted nudes on the neckties. They all have a certain rank honesty, an American flavor, like horseshit in a barnyard. You can respect it, because it's only itself, sweating away with no deodorant, gone hairy with no dipilatory and if some of the sad and sordid shops specialize in blown-up boobies, there isn't any real attempt to deceive, it's like more of a sad and sorry effort to make the sad and simple dreams of man come true.

But behind these petty putrescences sulks silently the sibilant shame of Shubert and Sulzburger: Ochs, du leper!

That might be like better if I broke the phrases, left out the punctuation and maybe like put "horseshit" in capitals, but you can't rewrite, it just clouds over the primal impulse, coagulates the flow of direct expression with the bankrupt tricks of craftsmanship. To put the finger on Ingers: Drawing is the obloquy of art.

UP FROM THE UNDERGROUND YEN

But, man, the absolute most in the way these squares box us in is at the Museum of Modern like Art. Not long ago they had a late-afternoon-early-evening kind of thing going on so a coterie of us wandered on up. What they were doing was blowing up scale models of the Parthenon, St. Peter's in Rome, Buckingham Palace, the Washington Monument, and the Metropolitan Museum of Art. It was a gesture of sympathetic interest in philosophic revolution and it sounded good to me. In addition to which it was the number-one pioneering effort in the aesthetics of dynamite. I guess there was something on it in Mussolini's invasion of Ethiopia in the old days, but those guys were all fascists, which

is about as square as you can get, unless you're Uncle Ezra, so the Abyssinian Abysm hardly counts.

Up at the museum, on the other hand, the dynamiter and the whole staff were thoroughly non-committed. The artist, under thirty-five, was a Californian, who'd studied in New York and had a Fulbright, a Guggenheim, and a Ford Foundation bonanza to work up the big bang. He'd been to Europe and interviewed some of the real old-time anarchists, the bomb throwers of yore. All this was in the catalogue with like statements from the Hercules Powder Corp.

It was a blast.

You get off the subway and it's not so bad. I mean like Lexington Avenue still has a lot of the sweat and hair of the American thing, but then you're crossing Park with not only the sweet Miestery of Life all over the place, but uptown, as far as the eye can see, the sterile apartments of the very rich. Very depressing. Another block and you're on, of all places, Madison Avenue. And not only Madison, but Madison at the end of the day. The street is crawling with copywriters and account executives and heady with the mortuary smell of deodorants.

THE AFFLUENT SOCIETY

Then, in a climax of impotence, you're on Fifth, the last and the worst. There's the engulfed cathedral, with all the phony Gothic on the outside, a stuffed model of Pius XII on the inside, and Cardinal Torquemada urging the faithful to bomb the Trans-Lux. There's a hundred depraved department stores corrupting the sheened-up, frozen women. There's Rockefeller Center where the word and the picture go forth on waves of air to hypnotize Oh America the spoiled toilers of the deep and even more the toilers of the shallow seduced and deflowered by electronics untouched by human hand man woman and child alike the victims of the sell game hard soft long and loud she sells see-sells everyone tarred with the same pitch oh my country and beyond in the tumescent twilight the towers of Time where soi-disant Republicans play fast and Luce with Life with Fortune and with Sacred Honour oh my star-spangled rectum retching at the thought you stagger lonely as a crowd through the revolving doors into the museum the last refuge of an honest man where the women come and go talking of Dr. Frankfurter.

That's how it looks with no punctuation at all. I'm still not sat-

The Sheened=up,
frozen women

isfied but I refuse to change it. Who wants commercial success?

Well, the big blast was out in the garden, naturally, and out we went. It was a shocker all right. I'd never been there at that time before. I usually come in through the Whitney where I pick up somebody's return ticket. The museum in the cool of the evening is quite different from the museum in the heat of the day. In the first place there's practically nothing there but squares in three-button black suits, some of them even have black ties, and they all look like they read the Cincinnati *Inquirer*. They're accompanied by their low-cut, bouffant ice cubes and everybody's belting into the martinis while the Mad Bomber's having trouble at the switch. I'm sloping around looking down powdered backs in deliberate preference to the well-structured mammalary attractions up front.

THE FLATULENT SOCIETY

The Washington Monument finally went off like a flaming phallus and as it did I heard one big space-buyer tell another there was a gold mine in this. Before the poor artist had got his fuses connected for Buckingham Palace, the space-buyers had figured a whole line of exploding architecture, from a schoolhouse for the kiddies to a de-luxe landscaped Hyde Park for their own employers. They even scheduled a model of Radio City for people who don't like television. I left the garden with the Parthenon falling into rubble behind me. There was polite applause.

I walked through the rain all the way back to the pad. As I walked it occurred to me that it had all been a ghastly mistake, putting the museum up there with the squares. The theory was fine. The theory was the squares would lose their corners. It wasn't working out that way at all. The squares, the cubes, and the poly-hedrons were all moving in, appropriating for their suburban jun-gles the finer things in life. This, I reflected, was even worse than the action-painting-by-the-numbers kits they had in the Bleecker Street Woolworth's.

THE WELL-WROUGHT YEARN

It was late when I got back to the pad and when I got there there was Estrellita lying on the floor, the last few ounces of deep red life pulsing out of her wrists.

She was real gone.

She'd done it with an old razor I hadn't used in so long I'd for-gotten I had it. Trust Estrellita to dig up the buried past. She was one good hustler, that girl, and I was sorry to see her go, but you couldn't blame her. All she wanted was a little integrity, just a sliver of honesty in her humble life and she was denied it. The agency vice-presidents had seen to that. In all her short life she had never found a bar without a situation comedy or a fixed wrestling match pounding away at her.

I knew there'd be questions. I knew I'd have to find a phone and call up some bureau somewhere. But first I just sat there with Estrellita. I got out a bolt of unbleached linen and my old pair of hedge shears and started a new composition, *Estrellita Perdita*.

I thought of her hunger for integrity and how we all have that hunger and I thought if I just wrote that down all in capital letters it would look like a telegram and the message would get through. But then I thought you'd have to press down the shift key and the shift lock and it would all be premeditated and cheap.

Olivetti had seen to that.

X
A POLICEMAN'S LOT

NOTE:

THIS SAMPLE was obtained at the weekly press conference of the chief of the Federal Bureau of Identification. Press conferences generally are a good source for our research, but this one was especially valuable because of its unusual feature of having no question period.

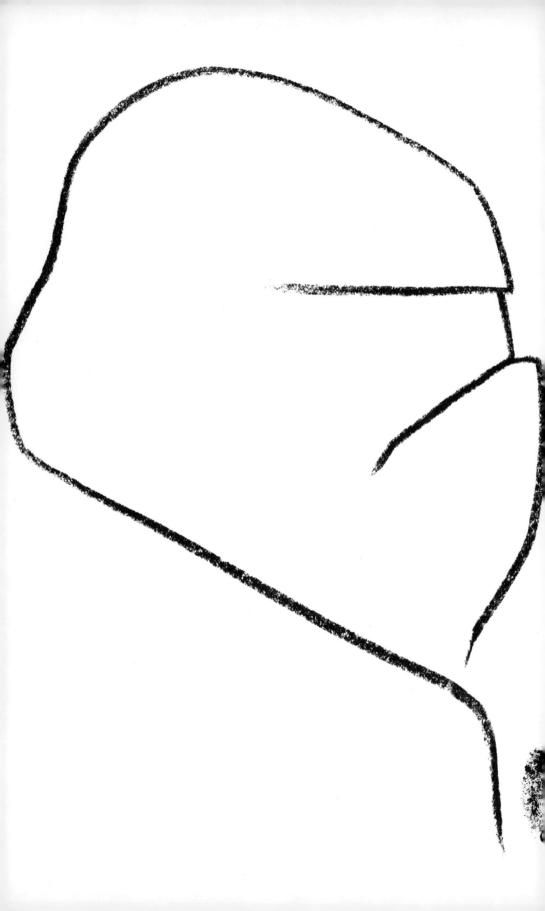

X

A POLICEMAN'S LOT

ROM AN outsider's point of view, or even on the basis of our own time-expenditure records, the impression can be gained that the chief demons facing the Bureau these days are of two classes, the JDs, as we call them in the Bureau, or Juvenile Delinquents, and, on the other hand, the Commies.

In point of actual fact, however, there is a third demon, or a third classification of demons, to speak more precisely, and this third demon actually gives us more trouble than the other two put together. If it were not for the third demon, the other two would have been handled effectively once and for all many years ago, about the time we were writing finis to the careers of those demons of the time Pretty Boy Floyd and John Dillinger. There is more than a little reason to suspect a secret underground connection among *all* the demons; if that working hypothesis turns out to be correct, there is little doubt in the minds of most law-enforcement officers that the kingpin of the whole underworld hierarchy, the directing genius behind organized crime and subversion in the United States, will turn out to be neither the Commies nor the JDs, but the Third Demon.

THE THIRD DEMON

The Third Demon—and I say this fully aware of the opposition it will arouse in some quarters—is what we call, at the Bureau, the Bleeding Heart. Other widely accepted names are the So-Called Liberal and the Pseudo-Intellectual.

In some quarters—not the same quarters as those just referred to from which opposition may be expected—the Third Demons are alluded to as the Self-Styled Civil Libertarians, and in

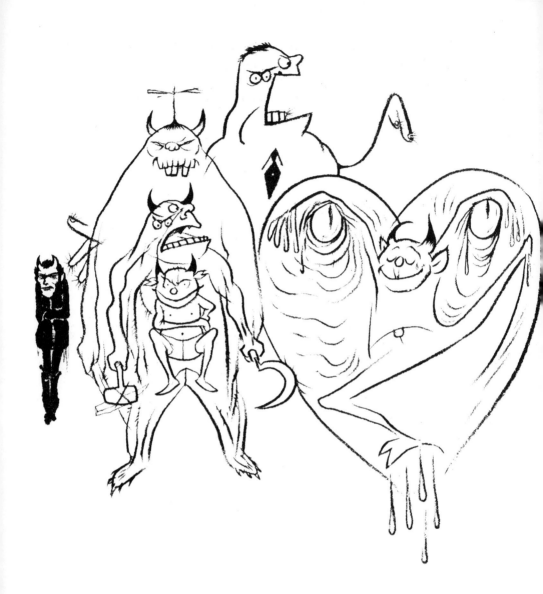

still others—quarters, that is—as the Militant Bill-of-Rightists, though that term should be discouraged because of possible confusion arising from the use of "Rightist" as a short form.

Finally, I have before me a report that among themselves members of this category employ the title *soi-disant intelligentsia*, which would certainly fit in with their general dislike of things American, even the language.

However, this hasn't been checked out yet, nor translated, for that matter. I offer it as an example of the gleanings the Bureau has in its "raw" files, material that can be invaluable to the law-enforcement officer but that it would be highly improper to reveal to the Congress, with its well-known connections to the press, and even more improper to reveal to persons being judged in the light of those "raw" files, since those persons are likely to be the very persons our whole effort is concerned to hold within bonds, or bounds, as the case may be.

DIFFICULTIES ON THE JD FRONT

The road blocks thrown in the path of the Bureau by the Bleeding Hearts—some of whom, I daresay, are motivated by what they regard as the best of intentions—are easily illustrated by the difficulties we encounter on the JD, or Juvenile Delinquent, Front.

Juvenile Delinquency is almost entirely a phenomenon that occurs in the city, the big city. Significantly, New York City has the highest concentration of Juvenile Delinquents in the entire nation, mostly located on the West Side. To us at the Bureau it does not seem wholly without significance that New York City also has the highest concentration of Bleeding Hearts in the nation. Even though the Bleeding Hearts tend to be located on the East Side—along with the United Nations—it is difficult to believe there isn't some subterranean connection besides the Shuttle, an excellent place, I may say in passing, to observe Commies passing information back and forth.

Now the remedies for JD are simple, clear, and plainly understood by all law-enforcement officers in the land. I need not go into detail, but psychologists—among the goriest of the Bleeding Hearts on this question—claim that JD activity merely indicates a desperate desire on the part of the individual JD for attention. To which we at the Bureau say, Let's give him the attention he deserves, fast, often, and with full vigor. I need not go into detail.

Against the application of this common-sense remedy for a situation that has become frankly intolerable, the Bleeding Hearts erect a whole interlocking structure of laws, institutions, and an organized effort to arouse public sympathy for the JD who wishes to assault the public rather than for the law-enforcement officer whose job it is to protect the public. Prominent in this structure are such antiquated notions as the old-fashioned prohibition against "cruel and unusual" punishment. I tell you frankly, I lay it on the line, we are up against a cruel and unusual class of youth criminals and something had better be done.

THE TRUMP CARD

The chief obstacle the Bleeding Hearts have erected to halt the Bureau's efforts to deal with the JD problem is the definition of almost all JD activity as offenses against the state or even against the municipality. This fractures the problem into forty-eight—or fifty, as we say now—fragments and sometimes into many times that number of splinters.

Until we can get the co-operation of Congress in placing all JD material under our own jurisdiction, the Bureau is forced to play its trump card on every occasion. This consists of an article written by me on JD and published in the magazine section of the Sunday *Herald Tribune*. This magazine section is particularly good because it appears as the supplement for many newspapers across the land. Thus our message gets into the homes of parents, congressmen, do-gooders and other molders of public opinion. I write this article for the *H T*, as we call the paper in the Bureau, once every fourteen days. It appears on the even-numbered weeks of the year.

ANOTHER TRUMP

On the odd-numbered weeks I write my piece on the Commies. Here again, the piece itself is the spearhead of our effort, but unlike the JD piece, which has to fight singlehanded, the Commie piece is backed up by existing laws and by concerted action on the part of the entire Bureau. Thanks to the sympathetic interest of the American people, we have managed to circumvent the Bleeding Hearts in dealing with the Commies.

It is, I suppose, an open secret that our chief device, second only to the fortnightly piece itself, has been infiltration. For years we have been infiltrating the Commie party and the various front organizations. We have been doing this with ordinary, patriotic Americans, housewives, reporters, truck drivers, and others, rather than with full-fledged agents. As a matter of fact, there's only one agent active full-time on the Commies and he's the man who deals with the *H T*.

The arrangement is simple. The volunteer infiltrator gets book rights and first-serial rights; residual rights go to the Bureau or to me, if the material happens to fall within some field I'm working on at the time.

The infiltration program has been so successful in attracting ambitious literary talent that as of this moment, according to reports on my desk, the entire active membership of the Commie party—CP, we call it—is working for the Bureau. As you can imagine, this situation leads to some pretty funny incidents at times. But it gives us total control over a potentially dangerous enemy of America. Anyone wishing to overthrow the government of the United States by force and violence—unless he's just a crackpot—has to deal with the Bureau. Just to be on the safe side, we've established dummy offices of the Syndicalists, the Anarchists, and the Nihilists, and, in Milwaukee, Wis., a one-man branch of the old I.W.W.

A QUESTION OF PHILOSOPHY

One of the most gratifying things to me personally about the infiltration program is what it does to the Bleeding Hearts. From time to time this segment of the community gets itself all exercised with petitions and collections and meetings in Madison Square Garden about some Commie whose rights are being infringed upon by the law-enforcement officers. But all unbeknownst to the Bleeders, the Commie is actually one of our infiltrators. We have many a hearty chuckle about this down at the Bureau.

What it comes down to, basically, is a question of philosophy. The Bleeding Hearts, in their muddleheaded way, are trying to fence us in by such things as allowing us freedom of action only *after* the crime has been committed. We Americans have a proverb about that. It has to do with whether to lock the barn door before or after the horse has been stolen. Today all of medicine is shifting its approach from the cure of disease to the prevention. Criminal investigation can do the same thing if given half a chance. With recent electronic advances both in the collecting and the classifying of information, the Bureau is within technicological grasp of the ancient ideal of the law-enforcement officer: to know for certain at every moment of the day what every member of the community is up to.

It will be the decision of the American people whether we push on to become a truly law-abiding country or, with the Bleeding Hearts, continue the present untidy state of things with all its loose ends.

In this general context, I should make clear that no one has more respect for the men who wrote the Bill of Rights than the men of the Bureau. But the fact is that Jefferson lived in a relatively primitive age, one in which even the concept of total surveillance would have been difficult to arrive at. There is no question but that the citizen ought to be protected from primitive police efforts that almost automatically make mistakes. But when, through electronic advances and through the sheer cultivation of enforcement-sensitivity, the possibility of error can be eliminated, then the whole question is a different one. It is to confuse the issue to pretend that times have not changed.

THE LAST TRUMP

The Bleeding Hearts have been confounded by the success of our infiltration program, but they have not, as yet, been permanently disposed of. Meanwhile, at the Bureau, we know from our "raw" files what the next major assault is to be. The target will be no other than the Bureau chief. It will be alleged that fifty years is too long a time for one man to direct law-enforcement activities. The names of Casey Stengel and of Otto von (Dropping the Pilot) Bismarck will be invoked, while Adenauer, De Gaulle, and Grandma Moses are conveniently forgotten.

Let me say in advance that whether I stay or whether I go, I will not negotiate or bargain. I don't really need the job. I've never gotten that much of a kick out of writing.

I can always go back to detective work.

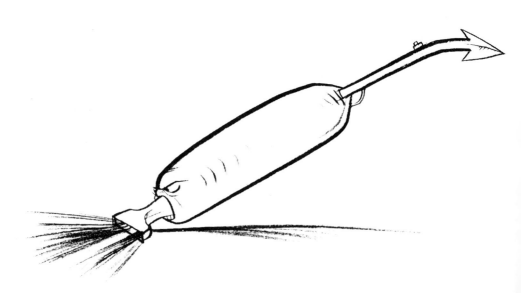

XI
THE UNMADE IMAGE

NOTE:

THE THOUGHT in arranging for the following transcription was that a first-class practitioner of public relations would be in an excellent position to survey a whole complex of areas otherwise unrelated. As things turned out the practitioner, or "counselor," had an impressive collection of demons of his own, peculiar to his field and virtually invisible from any other point of view. To obtain this valuable material, the research assistant merely telephoned and identified herself as a research scholar. Immediately an appointment was set up at a restaurant called The Four Winds, a ritual gathering place for the profession. After about three hours of what, when we analyzed it at the laboratory, we could only call trivia, the discourse became relevant.

XI
THE UNMADE IMAGE

. . . at least the original muckrakers had something specific to
rake up in the muck. Spoiled beef is no joke and neither are adul-
terated drugs. There was a goal for that old muckraking: the
Federal Food and Drug Act. Good idea, and, incidentally, good
public relations. Should have had it years before. But what is it
these people want? To pass a law against public relations? Out of
the question. The effort would take the expert services of too
many public relations men.

Let's face it: if these writers knew anything at all about public
relations, they wouldn't be writing about it, they'd be practicing it.

THE FREE PRESS AND THE FREE LOAD

All these carping critics are very strong on making the image
and manipulating public opinion and all that, but there's never
a word about the good things public relations men do for the
country. It's high time public relations had better public relations.
Actually we're making important contributions to the general welfare, but no one knows about them because we only speak for
clients and the clients are always trying to pretend we don't exist
at all.

But look at the press. Can you imagine what the daily newspaper would be without public relations? It would hardly exist.
Advertising men—who are always trying to run us down too—
tell you that advertising is what makes the press possible. In a
way that's true. Ads provide the income that keeps the papers in
business. But income's not enough. You need stories to fill in the
space between the ads; that's where we come in.

Every day, all across this land, the public relations contact men go out into the offices of the American press, into the great metropolitan dailies and the country weeklies, to the wire services and the syndicated columnists. They bring with them the news you'll be reading the next day or the next week. They bring with them your freedom, since that freedom depends on a free press and the press depends on our handouts to stay in business.

Sex, I often think, is one of the most important things in life for most of us. Yet how many realize how much of their sexual experience comes from the determined efforts of the P.R. men to keep the press free? I would estimate offhand that in the stories brought to the press each day by that army of dedicated public relations men, about ninety-two per cent somehow are connected with a photograph of a pretty girl in a bathing suit. When it comes to making a contribution to the continuance of society, how fundamental can you get?

Finally, public relations supports the press through reporters. Reporters are often thought of as apprentice P.R. men and so they are, but they also play a much more direct role in maintaining the freedom of the press. Advertising does indeed subsidize the press through the big spending brought on by the fifteen-per-cent-commission system of the agencies. But a more immediate subsidy is that donated by reporters in the form of low wages. This condition of theirs makes reporters particularly receptive to free drinks, free meals, big parties, and little mementos of happy relations. Many a front-page story begins when a reporter on the take meets P.R. on the make.

IS PUBLIC RELATIONS A FORM OF ADVERTISING?

Public relations is usually thought of as an adjunct of the business and industrial community. It is that, of course, but I and many practitioners like to feel that we play a somewhat more civic-minded role in the total community than, say, our brothers in the advertising business. Their only function is to push the product, to get out there and sell. I think they themselves realize the difference and that realization is behind the rather resentful attitude toward public relations often encountered among ad men.

We in the profession, on the other hand, are more concerned with the relatively intangible task of creating and maintaining a friendly feeling for the client and, by association, for his product.

Unless the reader or viewer of an ad actually buys the product, the advertising man has failed. We in public relations count our efforts successful if they simply induce in the audience a warm, pleasant feeling toward the client. Sometimes, indeed, we are successful if our efforts simply avoid creating antagonism.

WOMEN AND CHILDREN FIRST

In no area of American life can we take more justified pride in our work than in our tremendous contributions to the prosperity of traditional American institutions.

I'm not talking about persuading clients to write out a check for the Red Cross. That's important too as long as the local Red Cross people understand it is the practitioner who has activated the gift. I'm thinking rather of such things as the clubs and societies formed by the American Woman to occupy her leisure hours, of which, in each day, she has approximately twenty-four: In chronicles of times past we read about women similarly situated and, while we sympathize, we can hardly approve of the activities they chose for themselves. They were solitaries to a large extent and when they broke their solitude it was generally to commit adultery.

How much happier things are today! The modern woman of leisure is never alone long enough to form a dangerous liaison. For this we must thank her clubs and activities and they in turn must thank public relations. American Woman's husband, as industrial executive, frequently makes his public relations counselor available to his wife's organizations, whereupon they go into high gear. More directly, public relations has created complete programs, from illustrated lectures on detergents to seminars on beauty care, all designed to keep today's clubwoman wholesomely occupied. In exceptional cases we have even brought whole women's clubs into existence to achieve some special end, often legislative, and these, as you might expect, are the most active of all.

With children, too, the profession has been no less a source of rich benefits. Not to speak of educational films turning the minds of the young toward the paths of enlightened consumership, not to speak of the carloads of free balloons and bubble-gum that annually add a sparkle to a child's smile, let us consider, only, the profession's contributions to today's youngster as a social being or, as he has been called, the Organization Kid.

BOONE BOOM

With woman's life so thoroughly and so admirably organized, it follows that the children's lives must follow the same patterns, particularly in this age of rising pay and a shrinking force of domestic servants. If a woman is out on her rounds when school is over for the day, some provision must be made for the children or they will come home and wreak heaven only knows what damage on the accouterments of gracious living.

Hence, children's organizations. Also, of course, as preparation for their own adulthood. Noting only that public relations has created out of nothing the entire Little League movement as a place where the Organization Women can watch their Organization Kids in action, I should like to speak most fully of the Boy Scouts of America and of their upgrading due to public relations.

This estimable organization came into being, as nearly as I can discover, like most youth organizations as a course of study in skills and attitudes that would be useful when the child became an adult. Thus, the child was taught how, if lost in the woods, he could find his directions from the moss and the stars, he could build a fire to keep himself warm, and he could leave messages of stones for any search party out looking for him.

Clearly such skills were invaluable in the primitive society that gave birth to the Scouts. Without such skills the young boy once lost would have been lost forever, chilled to the bone, unguided and unheard from.

BEARD BORED

Times changed, however. The modern child does not get lost in the woods for the excellent reason that there are no more woods. If he is cold, he turns up the thermostat. If he has a message he calls up the recipient on the telephone and there are even cases of adolescents of both sexes using that device when they don't have a message.

For quite a few years, therefore, the Boy Scouts languished for lack of a purpose beyond the sale of brownish clothing and the endless impediments that hook on to belts and straps. Into this organizational vacuum came P.R. with its healing balm. Before you could say, Skit, Scat, Scout, we had those little waifs lined up and making field trips to the factories of our clients. They're still at it and there is no indication they will ever tire of it. As usual in our profession, everybody benefits: the boys are kept occupied, their mothers don't have to worry about them and the P.R. man, at the end of every month, has an impressive figure of visitors to show the client.

In the age of automation now dawning, it may even be that someday soon the only voices heard in the great production centers will be those of the touring Scouts, saying "Oh," and "Ah," and "Where's the toilet?"

THE IMAGE EMPHATIC

It may be, too, that the age of automation will bring on the greatest challenge and the greatest opportunity the profession has ever faced.

Any public relations man worth his salt will tell you—in strict confidence—that the greatest hazard to his work is the client himself. It is not only that the client is basically suspicious of public relations and is constantly looking for "results"—hence the value of all those Boy Scouts—but even more fundamentally, the client would not have hired a P.R. man in the first place unless he needed him and he wouldn't have needed him if he weren't such a thoroughly reprehensible character himself. Stingy, usually, wholly centered in his profits and production, the type with a knack for attracting the hostility of customers, colleagues, competitors, and employees with complete impartiality.

The trouble is that although this is true, and he knows it's true or he wouldn't have hired us, he nevertheless wants to dabble in P.R. himself, either proposing inexpensive projects that shout their cheapness to the world, or vetoing the most imaginative schemes the practitioner can come up with, and always on the grounds of cost.

Dickens managed to turn Scrooge into a kindly old gentleman, but Dickens was a great literary artist and no P.R. man is Tiny Tim. You break your heart building the Santa Claus image—far and away our most popular model—and every time the unreformed Scrooge sticks his head out from under the beard and spits on the public you've related him to.

Automation is our big chance. You can't automatize public relations—it's an instinct. But you can automatize management decision-making. When management is a machine, we can still be there, feeding the input and guiding the output. Then at last we'll have an image worth making. . . .

XII
REVEILLE FOR
REACTIONARIES

NOTE:

THE FOLLOWING is a transcript of an address at a private $1000-a-plate dinner held after the 1960 election by the Friends of the Republic, a political study and action group. The tape was made by the director himself, the only member of the Demonology Department old enough to seem a likely Friend or a likely diner at such a well-laid table.

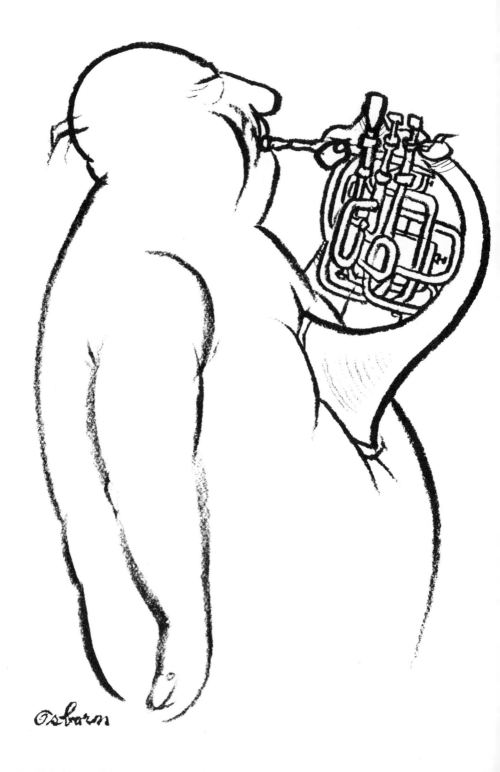

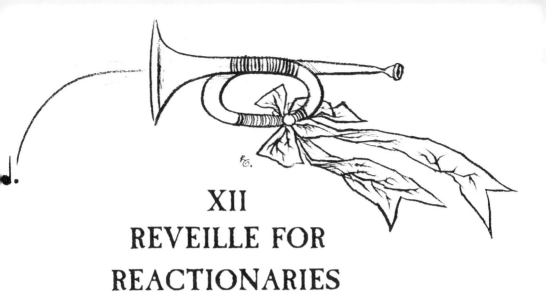

XII
REVEILLE FOR
REACTIONARIES

𝕴 TAKE IT we are all in agreement that a sizable majority of the American people are conservative at heart, want a conservative government, and will vote for a conservative President any time they get the chance.

These truths being self-evident, we must face the repugnant fact that, in 1960, the American people elected a liberal candidate and turned down our own offering. Furthermore, projections of present political alignments in the states make it all too clear that that performance will be repeated again and again except when we can get a non-political—and therefore non-conservative in any real sense—figure to head up the party's ticket.

How can these two opposing sets of apparent truths be reconciled? Or, to come down off the high plane of philosophy and into the realm of the practical, how can we manage to get elected again? To this question I shall address myself tonight.

O'ERLEAPED

In the first place, I think we must face squarely the fact that we are ourselves largely responsible for the liberal victory of 1960, and the resulting distress we now find ourselves in nationally. Our responsibility goes back to the heady year of 1947, when we found ourselves, for the first time since Hoover, in control of Congress. I shall not rehearse the genuine accomplishments of that Congress; they are too well known, sometimes I think much too well known, to need repetition. But gentlemen, we stooped to folly in backing the Twenty-Second Amendment to the Constitution, which forbids a President to succeed himself more than once.

As usual, we were acting from the highest of motives. We wished not to take our long-overdue revenge on Franklin Roosevelt, but rather to record for history the country's *real reaction*—hidden by the one-sided majorities he received in elections—to Roosevelt's career. What we all forgot was that Roosevelt was already dead and beyond the reach of our punitive action, except for post-humous impreachment, which, you remember, failed to get a majority in the party caucus.

Well, here we are: we've saved the country from Roosevelt but we've also saved it from ourselves. Without the Twenty-Second Amendment and with the astonishing geriatric advances being made by modern medicine—by free enterprise, conservative medi-cine—we might have successfully run Eisenhower for another twenty-five years. And in that time, surely *someone* else would have turned up.

POUR LE SPORT

As I've traveled about the country since the recent disaster, party workers everywhere have asked me if I think Mr. Eisenhower's golf had any effect on the election. I am afraid it did. No one can ever tell me the the American people will resent a leader who shares their own wholesome interest in sports, but golf may have been a mistake. To be sure, in the past, golf beat tennis handily. Surveys have shown that this was due to what people interpreted as the "special" nature of tennis. More people of voting age play golf than tennis; but the thing that escaped us is that most golfers play on public links, on a per-game basis. We undoubtedly carried the country club vote, but there is sound reason to think we could have carried that vote with mahjong—a game that, incidentally, might just have brought out the silent conservative majority. The total golf vote is more complex and may well have gone for the liberal candidate, especially in view of the universal experience of American youth with touch football.

My own feeling is that what we really need the next time out is a damn' good bowler.

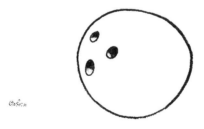

THE PRESS GANG

The foregoing observations have been necessary and, I trust, salutary reminders that to err is human and that we ourselves—

whatever the opposition may say—are human. We have made errors and they must be rectified. But actually, there seems little doubt that our consistent record of defeat at the hands of the liberals can only be due to the operation of demons in the republic. Demons are at large among our opposition, among their labor support and even among the electorate. While self-examination is called for every time we lose, we but deceive ourselves if we ignore a strong demonic element behind those losses.

It has been suggested by some that there are demons loose in the American press. I agree. But I do not share the view that the press demons operate most effectively among reporters and commentators covering the candidates. There seems to be no reason for doubting the view held by most of us that most American newspapermen are liberal themselves and unquestionably lend a liberal coloring to their reports. But after all, we do have this end of things covered. If reporters are liberal, their employers are, almost to a man, conservatives. If the reports are filed from a liberal point of view, they are actually printed from the point of view of the publisher who pays not only the reporters, but the editors, the copyreaders, the rewrite men, and the typesetters. The newspaper publishers of America are among our most loyal supporters. It would be base ingratitude to hit them where it hurts. Yet the only way to change the liberal thinking of most reporters would be to raise their pay, a dangerous innovation that might or might not help the party but that would certainly injure the party's publishers.

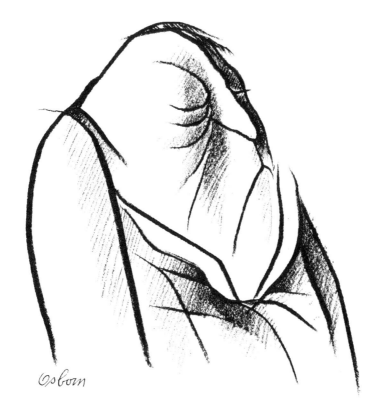

Osborn

Nor can I seriously entertain the notion that demonic reporters can be effectively disciplined by the loss of their employment. In the unlikely event that they really did leave the profession, they would all join journalism schools, where their ultimate influence would be multiplied many times. A much more probable outcome would be a grand shifting around, with the same men ending up on the same assignments for different employers only more embitteredly liberal for the move.

Closer examination reveals the demons of the press to be massed and most effective at the other end of the business, the consumers. Analysis of the returns shows city after city in which the voters, from sheer perversity, cast their ballots directly opposite to the way they were instructed by the press. This tendency was especially strong in those cities where both papers are published by the same member of our party's National Committee.

Difficult as it will be to all, there is only one solution. We must persuade a sizable proportion of our publishers to adopt the liberal line and thus get newspaper readers as antagonistic to liberalism as they are now to conservativism.

YES, WE ARE COLLEGIATE

In the excitement of watching the closeness of the popular vote in the 1960 election, some members of the party have come out for reform of the Electoral College. Some have even come out for the abolition of the College, backing the harebrained scheme of having the President elected by the majority of the voters.

I cannot warn you strongly enough against this madness. If we start going in for direct, popular election, the party is finished—at least until we can solve the master political riddle of our century, how to get the conservative majority to vote. You are all aware that we are more or less a permanent minority in both houses of Congress. We would be a much smaller minority if seats in that body all represented the same number of voters. On the other hand, we manage to maintain at least a veto power in most of the state legislatures: that too rests firmly on the lucky fact that the votes of country conservatives are worth from twice to four or five times the votes of liberals in the cities. Regardless of an occasional presidential fluke, the last thing in the world we can afford is electoral reform. Cling to the College; if possible make it even less representative of the people's voice than it is. That way lies our only hope until the conservative majority can be lured to the polls.

At last we must come to the real demons who defeated us in the late unpleasantness. These are, of course, the labor bosses and their organized minions scattered through the big cities and the heavily industrialized areas. The bosses have been after us for years. It is now apparent that for the last half-dozen elections their techniques have become more effective. The crux of the whole union strategy has been to get people to register and then to get them to vote. For some reason, the unions take it for granted that most people, if they vote at all, will vote liberal. They are right, of course, because the great conservative majority has simply been staying home on election day, in impressive but, alas, ineffective protest against the graduated income tax.

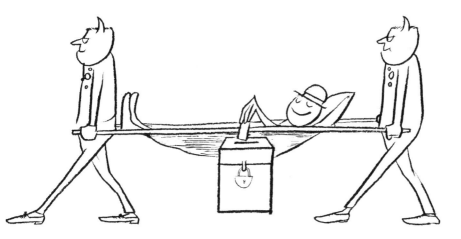

Against this vicious campaign of the unions to get people registered and voting, there is little we can do openly, since we are committed, through the advertising association, to the idea that voting is a patriotic duty.

What can be done otherwise is another matter. If, instead of aiming another blow at ourselves through electoral reform, we pushed electorate reform, we might be able to unfasten the grip the demons of the unions seem to have upon the voters. It has been mentioned by some party theorists that old Federalist thought included a property qualification for voters. Since some of our strongest supporters are not property owners in the strict, realty, Federalist sense, it has been proposed to restrict suffrage to those of a proper income. A dangerous proposal. I ask you only to compare the income of the average steelworker with that of the average bank clerk and ask yourselves who would suffer. The fact is that union labor—thanks to the outrageous annual demands upon industry of the union bosses—could meet almost any financial test we could reasonably propose.

What is really wanted is some way to forbid the vote to members of unions. In many a state legislature we have the votes to put such laws through and our lawyers are already studying the defense against the Supreme Court.

RO.

ARMAGEDDON

You understand, of course, that all these discussions of strategy are interim proposals. All become academic on the day we finally attract the conservative majority out of their political apathy and into the polls. On that day of wrath, even liberal dogcatchers —with their everlasting cant about finding the hound a home— will be swept out of office.

That day, as we have learned so often, is not yet. We cannot lose faith that it will come. I know that recent statistics of voting have been used to "prove" that the silent conservative majority does not exist. I say those statistics only prove that the conservatives are even more silent than we thought. When figures seem to show that almost all the voters have voted and that most of them voted for our opponents, those figures really mean that the conservatives have so lost heart that not only do they not vote, not only do they not register to vote, they do not even record the fact of their birth.

And who can blame them?

Osborn

XIII
THE LIBERAL DOUR

NOTE:

T HE FOLLOWING is a transcript of an address at a private Dutch-treat dinner held after the 1960 election by the Washington branch of Americans for Democratic Activity, a political study and action group. Attendance was limited to the inner echelon of the group. One of our younger researchers, by the simple expedient of spending three days addressing envelopes, had no difficulty gaining membership in that echelon.

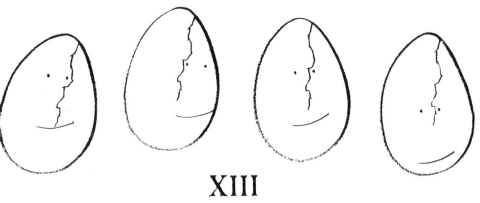

XIII

THE LIBERAL DOUR

THE LIBERAL program in America faces two fundamental, recurring problems: how to get elected and, having got elected, how to carry out the program.

The first part of the problem seems to have been solved, but we would be less than frank if we did not admit, at least to ourselves, that the very solution to the problem of getting elected has added immeasurably to the problem of putting the program into action.

The naive may ask, "How can this be?" They may wonder what it is, when a political party has received a mandate from the people, that can possibly stand in the way of executing that mandate. The political realist knows all too well.

YOUR PEOPLE, SIR, IS A GREAT BEAST

For the lamentable fact is that there isn't any mandate, there never was, and in all probability there never will be. The only popular mandate really received by a twentieth-century politician was the one given Adolf Hitler. Hitler said well in advance exactly what he was going to do; people voted for him to give him a chance to do it; once elected, he went right ahead and did it.

Things are different over here.

It's a good thing they are different and I wouldn't have it any other way, but the difference does make it difficult to plan ahead. Take FDR himself. We like to think that he had a mandate, that the people, ground down by the repressive policies of our opposition, rose in rebellion and voted in the NRA, the WPA, the AAA, and most of the rest of the alphabet. It isn't true. All those stirring events of the Hundred Days came up in the Hundred Days and not more than a week or two earlier. I think myself that people voted for FDR because he had a sculptural head and a voice to go with it.

People voted for Truman because *Life* magazine declared Dewey elected. And Eisenhower! Here the country was swarming with war veterans as never before; you would think the one thing they'd have in common would be a hatred of generals. Yet, in he

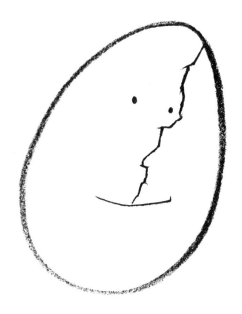

went, with tremendous majorities, not, I am positive, because people really wanted to rest and relax for eight years—which turned out to be his program—but only because he reminded them of Big Daddy.

Then we come to our recent triumph. Does anyone seriously imagine that it was the appeal of the platform that brought the thin margin of victory? I'll tell you what it was: it was the personal misfortune of our opponent that, under the hot lights of television, he sweat into his make-up.

No, the realistic truth is that the people are too damn' dumb to know what's good for them or even what they want. They are not demons, as some have suggested, but they are moved to and fro by demons of all descriptions as the grass in the field is moved by the wind. Our problem is not to build a platform with popular appeal, but to build a platform of our own and attach it to whatever does appeal, pre-eminently a political leader who doesn't sweat.

LOOK AWAY, DIXIE LAND

When we move from the people, victims of the demons, to the demons themselves, still inhabiting our society, we don't have very far to look. We don't even have to go outside our own party.

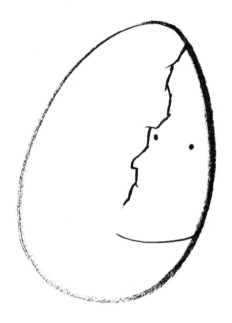

Foremost among the demons are the Southerners—by which, naturally, I mean the white Southerners.

It is at once the disaster and the salvation of liberalism in America that white people in the South still identify our opponents with Abraham Lincoln, despite the fact that Lincoln was a liberal if there ever was one. Consequently, when they go to the polls they vote, with basic unanimity, against Lincoln and for us. In presidential elections this automatically gives us a comfortable bloc of electoral votes. In the Senate and the House of Representatives the anti-Lincoln vote gives us normal party control of both houses. This is all to the good and ought to ensure the regular passage of liberal legislation in all fields.

Nothing of the sort happens. In session after session, liberalism proposes and the South imposes. When the chips are down the only thing we can really count on from the South is the quadrennial anti-Lincoln vote. The rest of the time, they're all Republicans, though they can't admit it. Actually, if the GOP changed its name—to Whigs, perhaps, or Anti-Federalists—and gave us Lincoln, Jacob Javits, and perhaps Nelson Rockefeller, they could carry the South tomorrow.

Happily, this is unlikely.

Osborn

Difficult as are the demons of the South, there's one thing to be said for them: they're down there and we're up here. This redeeming grace does not apply to the other great crew of demons within the party, the big city bosses of the North.

It's all very well to be sentimental and pretend that modern liberalism grew out of the old-time boss and his jobs for people's down-and-out relatives, grocery baskets at Christmas time, and an annual organization picnic up the river. This happens not to be true. The only thing that grew out of the old-time boss is the new-time boss and he's no improvement. He doesn't give a damn for liberalism or anything else. All he wants is to get his followers into jobs, both elective and appointive, and to run the city to suit himself. From time to time he uses the city to run the state and every so often he tries to use the state to run the country. The whole program of liberalism, to him, is a cheap modern substitute for the old-time grocery baskets.

By all the laws of history the city boss should have been dead and gone when such liberal programs as Social Security, unemployment insurance, and old-age assistance became a matter of law rather than patronage. Instead, he's stronger than ever. Not needing graft the way he used to, he's not even liable to investigation any more. He just goes around shaking hands with people

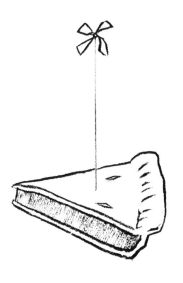

who shake hands with other people and they all vote as they're told. There's no discussion, there's no dialogue, there's no fruitful exchange of views.

How can you educate people for democracy that way?

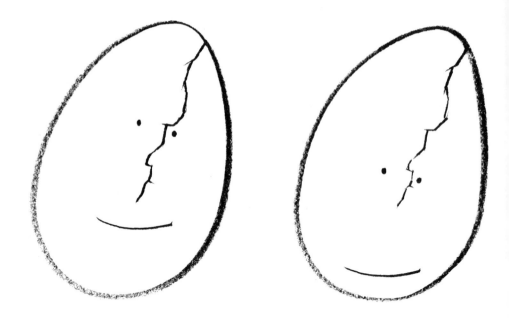

DEMONS INDEFINITE

When all the sins and shortcomings of the party are acknowledged, however, we are faced with the fact that the real demons are still those on the outside, members of the opposition or the financial and industrial power behind the opposition, the mill owners and monopolists of America. They're a slick bunch and you have to watch them every minute.

This shows clearly even in recent developments of what may be called the corporate silhouette. In days gone by the American industrialist was easy to recognize and natural to hate. He wore a high silk hat, smoked a big cigar, and had a great fat belly covered by a vest embroidered with dollar signs. This has all changed. Today's exploiter of the masses keeps himself in good physical shape, wears expensive but tasteful clothes, and is not immediately distinguishable from his better-paid employes. Worse still, he's had a decent education, reads books, goes to the theater, buys paintings and attends the opera to hear the music. This is protective coloration of the most deliberate sort and, I am sorry to say, it works.

Personal camouflage of this kind is only the surface manifestation of the same thing going on deep within the corporate labyrinths. One of the great burdens borne by liberals in America is that when we win we lose. Thus when we got minimum-wage laws

passed and people were able to earn enough to live decently, their first reaction was to vote Republican to show that they were respectable now. With industry and finance we've had the same bitter fruits of victory. Years ago, after frightful battles, we legislated a certain minimum of honesty into banks and factories. Do we get credit for this? No, today's money man, operating within the strict supervision we placed upon him, proudly proclaims his own honesty.

"I'm no scoundrel," he says, and people believe him because he's right. The point, however, is that his grandfather *was* a scoundrel

Osborn

and ought to be hounded for it until the means of production are in the hands of the people, that is to say, of ourselves.

It's quite true that during the lean years when Eisenhower reigned most of us moved out of the White House into the great foundations. The result is that the foundations themselves have taken on a strongly liberal cast, but the result of *that* is that people give credit, not to the tax laws that made foundations inevitable, but to the tycoons and operators who made all the money in the first place and who left their names inseparably linked with the loot for public purposes.

THE ROAD AHEAD

There is no doubt that the people really want liberalism in the years before us. Our task is to make them understand that they want it. As to the nationalizing of industry, we are already well along that path. Increasingly, industrial income is going into the foundations and increasingly the foundations are becoming a branch of the government—limited, so far, to information and analysis. The breakdown in Soviet-American friendship was a traumatic shock to many of us, but it may yet prove the vital occasion for the absorption of the few remaining areas of industry not already foundationalized.

We are thus confronted with the great obstacles to the liberal program: the party in the South and the party in the Northern cities. The only major sector of the party we're really sure of is the party on the campus and the trouble with the party on the campus is that most of the members aren't old enough to vote.

What we need above all is some way to keep the voting support of the city bosses and the Southern masses, but to keep both firmly out of policy making. Unless we are prepared to settle for the presidency of the student council, we must continue to use both, as in the past.

The emerging question of liberalism in America is, Who is using whom?

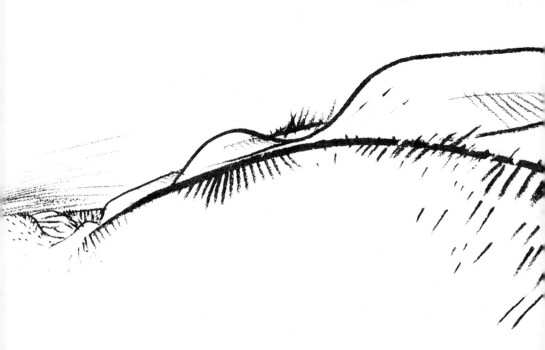

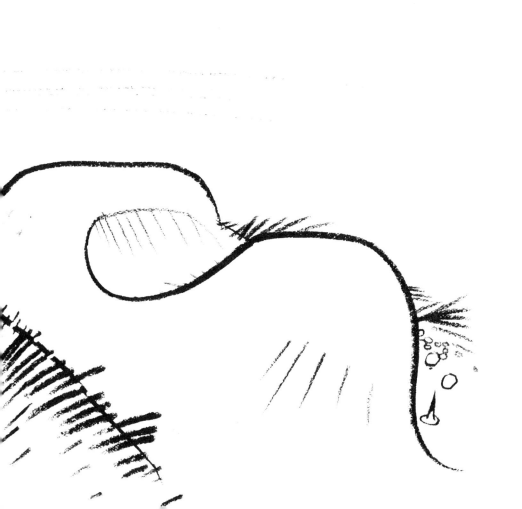

XIV
THE ELDERS OF ZION

NOTE:

AGAIN, THE bedrock necessity of diligence and ingenuity is illustrated. The researcher, convinced that the material was there, obtained employment as a bus boy in the executive dining room of the Middle Western headquarters of a well-known industrial giant. After ten laborious days he had his sample and was allowed to keep the tips.

XIV
THE ELDERS OF ZION

ITLER WAS an absolute madman. He plunged Europe and then the world into the most frightful war in history. He first ravaged the countries of Eastern Europe and then arranged, through his own ineptitude, that they should pass into Red control. The line between communism and capitalism is drawn through the heart of Europe; before Hitler, it was on the edge of Europe. He was also responsible for attaching a certain stigma, brief, perhaps, but humiliating, to some of the finest financial and industrial brains in Germany; he did this by obtaining their support, in money and in other ways; after the defeat of

Germany, the Allies, understandably but most unfortunately, tended for a while to regard with suspicion the leading citizens of the business community who had worked with Hitler in organizing Germany and the German provinces of Europe. But the poor fellows really had no choice. We did business with some of them before the war and do now, so I know what I'm talking about, they had no choice at all; it was either join the New Order or drastically curtail one's operations.

But of all the insane things Hitler did, the one with the worst and most lasting bad effects, everything considered, on balance, was his treatment of the Jews. In the beginning, I think his Jewish program gained a lot of sympathy among the better elements here and probably abroad too. But when the war was over and the world learned about the gas ovens and the concentration camps, there was a perfectly natural feeling of revulsion. As a result, what Hitler really did was to make simply impossible any rational, intelligent discussion of the Jewish problem.

A MATTER OF PROTOCOL

Other results of Hitler's extravagant Jewish policy may appear more important, but they are only more spectacular. The creation of the state of Israel, for example, was the direct result of Hitler's extremism, and many view the existence of that state as the direst threat to Christian civilization since Disraeli became prime minister of Britain.

It is not such a threat. The fact is the Arabs can wipe out Israel anytime they're allowed to. They very nearly did it during the so-called Suez Crisis of Anthony Eden. Israel, you will recall, acting through the pressure centers of international Jewry, persuaded Britain and France to invade Egypt under the guise of making Suez safe, but actually to make Israel safe. Almost immediately it became clear that the Egyptians were winning the war: they lured the Jewish armies deep into Egypt and were about to destroy them when the wily Israeli, again showing the fantastic international power of the Jews, maneuvered both the United States and the Soviet Union to intervene and save the Jewish state from destruction.

So the sons of the desert, fighters of old, are on guard and will destroy the noxious state when the time is ripe. Meanwhile Israel is protected by forces of the United Nations, which, of course, has been a Jewish front organization from its inception.

We don't really have to worry about Israel. It is, to be sure, a sanctuary for Jews fleeing from the just anger of mankind, but Jews have always found such sanctuary, whether in the stock exchanges of the world or in the government of the United States.

THE WHOLE MEGILLAH

But this business of free discussion being choked off by the idiocy of Adolf Hitler is very serious. The reasoning runs like this: Hitler killed millions of Jews; therefore, every ladies' ready-to-wear merchant in town should be welcomed with open arms into the Country Club. That's bad enough, but from the same premise you get even more outrageous conclusions: Hitler killed millions of Jews; therefore, we must not even discuss the growing power of the Jews, but must sit silently by while they take over the whole country.

They're doing it, too. Look at Connecticut. Did you ever think you'd see the day when the state of Connecticut had a governor named Abe Ribicoff? Our forefathers came out of Connecticut and the rest of New England to spread Christian civilization in the wilderness. We did it all right, but some of us should have stayed home to keep Christian civilization there.

Did it ever strike you that you don't hear many Jewish jokes any more? That's no accident. The Jews are in control of the entertainment business from top to bottom and one of them or a bunch of them made a definite decision to kill the Abie and Ikey stories as part of the general Jewish infiltration program.

They can talk all they want about television, but television, thank God, is still largely in the control of American industry. That's why, whatever else you may say about it, the programs are clean and wholesome. But look at the movies: one kootchie-kootchie spectacle after another. Look at the theater: all they can think about is some new form of sexual perversion. They haven't had a sick young hero who does it with sheep, yet, but they will, they will. That's Jewish art for you.

They get into everything. The doctors had to set up quotas in the medical schools or by today a woman couldn't have a baby without having it brought into the world by a Jewish doctor. In law, they've just about taken over the whole profession.

I wouldn't hire one of them. I wouldn't have one in the plant. It's cost me money, too, but it's a matter of real principle. We've had cases where the other side had a smart Jewish lawyer and we lost, but I'd rather lose like that. The plant has come a long way since I came into the factory. We have, for example, quite a number of Irish foremen now and I suppose my father would turn over in his grave if he knew that. But they've come along and you have to keep up with the times. Not the Jews. Every one of them is strictly out for himself and they stick together like sardines in a can.

QUELLE HUTSBAH!

They had togetherness patented before the women's magazines ever heard of it. Have you ever driven by the big new country club they built for themselves out north of town? The place looks like a resort hotel. They've got swimming pools and steam rooms, a better chef than you can find downtown, and I don't know what all. They like to live well. But the point is they're clannish. They have to have their own country club so they can get together and talk about the rest of us. It frightens me when I drive by the place.

I'll tell you what frightens me more, though, is the way they're getting into one decent neighborhood after another. It doesn't affect me one way or the other. I'm out in the country. I like it out there and you have to drive fifteen or twenty minutes to reach the next house. But every one of our top executive personnel and almost all the board members live in a neighborhood into which at least one Jewish family has moved in the last five or ten years. I know because I asked them. I'm not talking about real estate values or even the general tone of a neighborhood, although both those can be bad news to a property owner when the Jews start moving in. I'm talking about what it means. You multiply that situation all across the country and you have the Jews moving into the better residential areas and the better suburbs everywhere. That means they're putting their hands on more and more of the levers that run this country.

WHAT A SIMMIS!

Where do you find them? Do you ever run into a real industrialist who's a Jew? You bet your life you don't. The work's too hard and the profits are slow and steady. They all want to make a million fast and a lot of them are doing exactly that.

So they're in the entertainment business. That lets them lower the moral standards of the whole country.

They're in the banks. Thank God we still have some old-

*Why can't they
dress the way
we do?*

fashioned Christian family banks out here in the heartland, but I tell you, boys, in the East half the bankers you meet are Jewish. That means they control the vital flow of money and credit, which is the very blood stream of the economy.

They're in retailing. God, are they in retailing! They never want to make anything themselves. They just want to buy and sell the product of other people's brains and labor. That means they sit like a road block at the crucial point between producer and consumer, taking a toll from both and manipulating the laws of supply and demand any way they want.

They're intellectuals. There isn't a Jew you meet that doesn't read books and go to concerts. They have far more than their share of the writers, scientists, and philosophers. That's because they'd rather sit on their ass and think about things than get out and work. But what it means is that they're the people who teach the people who teach our children. No question about it, that's the origin of all this furor and court cases about morning prayers, Bible reading, and Christmas parties in the schools. Damn it all, the public schools were Protestant in origin and we have every right to keep them that way. The Catholics didn't like that, so— you have to give them credit—they went off and built their own schools, where they can say the Lord's Prayer without the Kingdom and the Power and the Glory.

Not the Jews. They want to move right in and take over the schools, throw out all religion. Or worse, bring in their own religion. You may not believe this, but last Christmas my own granddaughter started explaining to me what Channukah is. Do you know what Channukah is? It's the Jewish Christmas. Do you know where my granddaughter found out about it? In the public school! That did it for me. I told my daughter to take her out of there at once and put her in Miss Bield's, where she belonged anyway, and I'd foot the bill. Channukah in the public schools!

HEAR, O YSROEL

Finally, you find them in the labor unions. Not as working stiffs, needless to say, but in the top jobs, where they can tell American businessmen whether their factories will work or close. David Dubinsky! Jacob Potofsky! Their very names sound like bomb-throwing anarchists. I have to laugh at people like MacDonald and Reuther and that smart-aleck Carey. They think they're really big men and they throw their weight around, but someday they're all going to wake up and find out they've been working for the Jews all along. When the Jews are ready to take over they won't need people like that around. They'll just push the button in labor, push the button in the banks, push the button here, push the button there, and they'll own the United States. They already own Russia and that'll give 'em the world.

I know, I know, you know some fairly decent Jews. So do I. I'm not a bigot that tries to say every individual Jew is as bad as most of them. But the thing is, boys, a Jew is a Jew and sooner or later it has to come out.

I've been thinking about this a good many years and I've reached this conclusion: when all is said and done, however nice some of them may seem, they're just not Christian and that's all there is to it.

XV
DEMONS IN THE PLUTOCRACY

NOTE:

ANOTHER CONVENTION. This one at the permanent Atlantic City headquarters of the International Amalgamated Union of Hewers of Wood and Drawers of water, the powerful IAUHWDW. The sample comprised the president's greetings.

Osborn

XV
DEMONS IN THE PLUTOCRACY

IF THERE'S one thing that gets my ass out it's these hypo-critical millionaires and their silver-spoon sons that cry all the time for restrictions on the awful power of the unions. You know why the awful power of the unions came into existence? Because the god-damned millionaires are such complete crooks.

Yeah, yeah, everyone's forgotten all this, but those guys were bandits and they still are at heart and every time there's a dollar lying around they put the snatch on it. I tell you every union leader in the country would have to be not only totally crooked, he'd have to grab every cent of the union's money he could find and hop the first boat to Rio to have the graft and corruption in the unions begin to match the big steal put on over a period of a hundred years—Christ, it's still going on, only not as gaudy—by the millionaires of America.

Incorporated.

Die protestantische Ethik und der Geist des Rapitalismus

From the word Go they were and are a bunch of hymn-singing hypocrites out to put the knife in their neighbor before their neigh-bor put it into them. And the millionaire-type neighborhoods these robbers lived in, they were absolutely right. They stole from each other, they stole from the government, they stole from the public, and they stole from their own workers. Especially they stole from their own workers. They hired the Pinkertons to shoot up the workers and they ran company towns where every cent you earned was owed before you got it. They hired women because women were cheaper than men and they worked children because children were cheaper still. They'd be doing it yet if the unions hadn't got a law passed against it. And these cheap rich bastards have the nerve to stand up and plead for the right of the individual worker against the awful power of the union. What they're pleading for is the right of the individual worker to get screwed. They themselves are standing by, ready to do the job.

And every damn' one of them was a big man in the Sunday service department with Bless you, my children and Let us gather at the river for evensong. They couldn't get enough of gentle Jesus, meek and mild, and for every million they stole they'd put up a church and for every townful of workers they screwed they'd put up a chapel.

The actual living Jesus Christ said, and I quote, "It is harder for a rich man to enter the Kingdom of Heaven than it is for a camel to go through the eye of a needle." To you and me, brothers, those are words of one syllable and their meaning is clear. To the pious millionaires who worry about union power, those words meant something else. Their tame ministers got up every Sunday and told them what Christ really meant was the more money you got the more God loves you.

CATTOLICISMO E PROTESTANTESIMO NELLA FORMAZIONE STORICA DEL CAPITALISMO

Now brothers, you know the union stands against any kind of discrimination, whether it be on the grounds of race, religion, or place of national origin. Lest I be accused of being anti-Protestant, I hasten to point out that you can follow exactly the same pattern as described and sing *Tantum Ergo* instead of *Rock of Ages*. You all remember Bobbie the badger, the Senate investigator that tried to give us a hard time. Well, you know the family, they're all big touch-football players and they're all big Catholics—like the Pope only with more money. You know where Bobbie's Big Daddy got all the dough? He was a pure and simple dollar juggler in Wall Street, the last of the red-hot speculators. He just about was the last, too, in the old-time, Fancy Dan way. Because when he had everything in sight, he went straight and joined the Feds, setting up the Securities and Exchange Commission to put people in jail for doing what he'd spent his life doing.

So Bobbie's devoting his life to public service; so's Jack; so's Nelson for that matter and everybody thinks this is great. When

I was a kid I used to see old John D.—the mummy—in the news-reels handing out the shiny new dimes. The sons and the grandsons are still doing it only they got it better organized and no doubt the money is doing a lot of good for medicine and Latin America and higher education and so forth and so on, the only thing is, nobody ever suggests they give the money back to the people they stole it from in the first place.

My God and they call us Robin Hood; I'd rather they called us just plain hoods.

THE VOYAGE OF THE BEAGLE

Now if there's one thing these patriotic old con men are tops at, it's the fuller explanation complete with diagrams and pictures. In recent years they've been pouring the shiny new dimes into American scholarship and believe me American scholarship knows which side its dime is buttered on. American scholarship is grate-ful for those shiny dimes and American scholarship has come forth with the big explanation.

It's evolution.

That's what it is, evolution, just like the fish egg developing into the dinosaur and the dinosaur developing into Barry Goldwater. American capitalism and all those millionaires have been going through the big evolution and there's nothing to worry about, boys, because they stand upright now, just like human beings. They've lost their tails, their jaws have gone in, and their fore-heads up. They've traded in their shaggy fur for Brooks Brothers' latest and they all read the *Reader's Digest* like mad; they're a pretty cultured bunch.

Let me give you just the high spots of the evolution of American capitalism, or, Up from the Swamp. Sorry I don't have my graphs with me, but from what I read in the *Wall Street Journal*, there's too much graph in this union now.

LUCK AND PLUCK

The first stage is the Horatio Alger period. Our young hero, Bill the Bond-Salesman, is walking along Broadway, just minding his own business, looking for someone to stick with some more wall-paper. Suddenly there's a gasp from the crowd. Bill looks up and there, right in front of Father Duffy, is a runaway hansom cab and inside the cab, bouncing around like grapefruit in a landing net, is golden-haired Gloria, daughter of Jay Gould out of Hetty

Green. Bill rolls up a bundle of bonds, thrusts them into the horse's mouth, and saves the girl. The young folks are married and Bill goes into partnership with Gloria's uncle, Captain Kidd.

Needless to say, the villain of the piece, Dirty Dick the Driver, was a teamster handling the hack and he got the heave-ho on the spot.

WHAT IMMORTAL HAND AND EYE?

In the next phase of the drama of evolution, Bill enters in the guise of a sabertooth tiger. He eats up everything within reach and then begins increasing his reach. Presently there is nothing much left except the smile on the face of the tiger.

At this point a chorus of scholars arises in the orchestra pit. They speak: "It may look like robbery, but it's the creation of the American industrial plant. It may look like murder, but it's the filling out of our Manifest Destiny. It may look like the cheapest kind of swindle, the most heartless exploitation of child labor, the most ruthless war against free workers, but appearances are deceptive and the fact is this: the tiger owns both the police *and* the press, so sit down and shut up."

Blackout.

The ages grind along. Mountains arise, the waters recede, the climate changes. When the lights come on again the tiger is sitting in his office having a manicure. With his free paw, he picks his teeth with the leftover thigh bone of an early union organizer. He speaks: "Now that we've built the industrial plant of America, we can afford to be generous and kind. I'm going to raise pay all around, give the men job security and put doors on the toilets. I don't want to be a tiger any more, I want to be an industrial statesman."

Enter a committee of eminent medical men, smoking filtered cigarettes and dissolving aspirin in glasses of water.

From beneath his desk the tiger produces the tenderized corpse of Joe Hill, the greatest organizer of them all. "Gents," he says to the assembled sawbones, "I know you people in the medical schools need assistance and I want to contribute this first-rate cadaver." The doctors leave and the tiger sits musing on a pile of gold he keeps in the corner.

He speaks: "What good is all this gold to me, what good is all the power of industry, when there isn't freedom in the land? No good, that's what. Now that I'm an industrial statesman, Let's Bust the Unions!"

BRING FORTH THE FIFTH

Well, brothers, what can we do? Are we going to listen to all these industrial statesmen and the flower of the higher learning and then say, "Crap! Any concession you made to labor, to the public, or to common decency, you made only because somebody

R. Osborn

was sitting on your chest." No, brothers, that wouldn't be polite. Even without scholars, I think we're going in for a little of that evolution juice ourselves.

How does it work? Like this.

For the sake of discussion, let's say I'm a crook, I'm looting the union treasury and not practicing union democracy. Now formerly, I simply would have denied all charges. And by the way, if any of these statements turn up in congressional investigations, I tell you in advance I'll take the Fifth. I'll also take the First and I'll take the Fourteenth. I'd take the Eighteenth but somebody already took it.

Now, we simply admit everything. I'm a crook, a labor boss and the rest of you guys don't have any more democratic rights than the small stockholders in General Motors.

But, we say, this ain't bad, it's good. It's evolution and there's nothing we can do about it. Today a crook, tomorrow a labor statesman. You can't interfere with the inexorable march of evolution. It ain't historical. It ain't statesmanlike. It ain't healthy.

Comes the evolution, we'll all be Dubinskys!

In the meantime, brothers, let us now vote unanimously to accept the treasurer's report. Any brother who wants to read it can see me later, in my office at the end of the pier.

XVI
BAD MEDICINE

NOTE:

ANOTHER CONVENTION. This one was the American Medicinal Association, meeting on the Isle of Capri with expensible side trips to London, Paris, Rome, and what the management kept referring to as "St. Petersburg." Once again, the Director of Demonology made the tape himself rather than tie up the time of a graduate student. The speaker, a distinguished brain surgeon, was the Association's director of legislative relations.

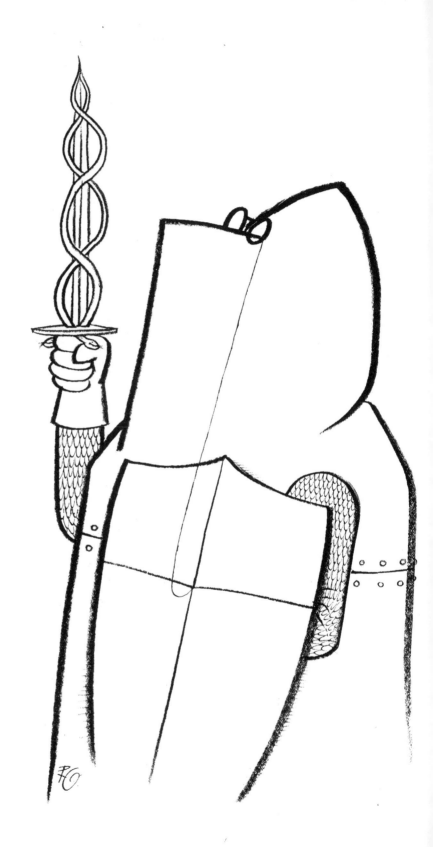

XVI
BAD MEDICINE

ODAY, GENTLEMEN, medicine faces its gravest crisis since the rise of chiropractic. Once again we are surrounded by demons. They are stronger than ever. They come at us from all directions. And, there is no use kidding ourselves, in recent years they have gained much ground and from these gains they are in a much better position to press their attack to its logical conclusion, namely, the death of organized medicine as we know it today.

The cry today is for medical care for the old folks. But you know and I know that medical care for the old folks will be but the prelude to universal health insurance for all, or socialized medicine.

HISTORY OF THE DISEASE

On the odd chance that there are among you some who doubt the inevitability of this sequence, let me remind the convention of my own humble and, I regret to say, futile part in warning the members against the early signs of the dread disease when first they appeared in the body politic and social.

The first symptoms, you will recall, were centered on the request for prepaid group insurance for hospital care. The whole thing was said to have no relationship at all to doctors but merely to be a helpful budgeting device for potential patients. Many in the profession, I am sorry to have to recall, were deceived by this plea and went along with the request. For myself and a few others, as soon as we spotted the word "group," we knew we were in the presence of socialism. We said so at the time, we have said so ever since, and we say so today. Anything that casts even the slightest shadow over the sacred relationship between the doctor and his patient's finances is socialism.

As we predicted, it was not long before the next stage set in: the impertinent demand that doctor fees too be insured against, as if we were some kind of natural disaster.

ACUTE ATTACK

Over our protest, the profession again acceded to the socialist demons. Rate schedules for doctors were set up, exactly like those for air travel or Caribbean cruises. Doctors were paid, not by the patient, but by the group, as if a group ever had consumption, vapors, or tired blood.

The key point, however, was that fees were known in advance. We were deep in trouble, but there was worse to come. The rate of progress of the disease became terrifying. First, there was treason within the profession. Young doctors, motivated by a false idealism, joined together in group practice. Even as the British rose to Benedict Arnold, demoniacal labor unions embraced these traitors. Unions built their own hospitals. They formed their own groups and pushed the whole insurance scheme into preventive medicine. Worst of all, they laid rough and untrained hands upon the very heart of the science of healing: they began the first study by outsiders of the costs of medical care.

Now the disease has reached its climax. Socialized medicine—under various more palatable names—is the avowed goal of wide areas of the population and even the government. If it comes—and we cannot be optimistic that it won't—the profession will be ruined. Bureaucrats will demand a fixed scale of prices. The frontiers of free enterprise will be fenced in. The advance of medicine will grind to a halt. I, for one, freely predict that, if we are socialized, many of the profession's brightest lights will return, in sorrow, to the mother trade, barbering, where at least they'll get tips.

DIAGNOSIS

One of our greatest problems is communicating our concern to our patients. "After all, what difference does it make?" is a question asked by people of good will and small brain. "Look at England," they go on, "surely the citizens there are better off medically than they used to be?"

Well may they say, "Look at England." Look at her! Every tatterdemalion lounger and loiterer in London sports a wig and a

set of false teeth, while the empire's gone glimmering after Babylon and Tyre. That's what socialized medicine's done for England!

What we have to get across to patients and to voters is the fundamental connection between the fee system and the march of medicine. Without fees, and big ones, too, there would have been no wonder drugs, no antibiotics, no tranquilizers, no Paul de Kruif. Once upon a time, you know, we had socialized medicine. When we were all barbers, we were thoroughly socialized, employees of the state in military or courtly service. What did you get then in the line of treatment? You got leeches and bloodletting generally. You got herbs and rare earths. You got the water cure. You got the phases of the moon. You got clysters of simply enormous sizes. The best thing a doctor could do for you then was to give you a shave and a haircut.

Two bits.

Just about what the treatments were worth. This system continued basically right into this century, with the doctor a kind of community functionary, handing out folk remedies to the folks and taking his pay in chickens and parsnips, much like the parson.

Abruptly, everything changed. The march of medicine began. We cured syphilis, typhoid, bubonic plague. We discovered allergies and psychoanalysis, two of the most fruitful fields a man can enter. Geriatrics, pediatrics, gynecology, and many others came out of the nowhere into the here, and mankind climbed steeply toward a new era of tranquillity. What brought all this on?

In a word: Cash.

GREAT MOMENT IN MEDICINE

When America moved from the country into town, people no longer had the poultry and produce they used to pay their doctors with. They had to pay cash. Doctors moved from the lower middle class to the middle middle class to the upper middle class. They got rich. And, as in every other break-through on the frontiers of free enterprise, from the spinning jenny to the singing commercial, the benefits filtered down from those on top, the enterpreneurs, to those on the bottom, the customers. For example, we have been so successful in fighting infant mortality that we've had to go in for birth control. Other beneficiaries are the oil-well business, the modern-art business, and the travel business; all have benefited enormously from the great strides of modern medicine.

This has happened because the fee system is solidly rooted in Nature herself. I daresay there isn't a doctor in the house who hasn't said to his patients, "We don't cure you; we only co-operate with Nature."

Nowhere is that co-operation more direct and more effective than in the therapeutic application of fees, based as they are on the patient's ability to pay, with just a touch added on top of that ability. It is precisely that touch, calculated with exquisite delicacy and applied with the inexorability of doom, that has made America the healthiest nation of its size in history. The constant presence of that touch activates Nature, and Nature, deep in the patient's subconscious, keeps him healthy most of the time and gets him healthy fast when he does fall sick.

CLINICAL DEMONSTRATION

The vital connection from Fee to Nature to Good Health is most easily seen in psychoanalysis. Say a patient comes in suffering from guilt feelings over having carnally desired his mother when he was two years old.

Well, the poor chap lies around the office, maundering on about this every Mon., Wed., and Fri., at $50 a "visit." The twilight afternoons go by; the seasons follow one another in the eternal return and, after a year or two, the man realizes that he's broke and has to get a job working nights to keep up the treatments. Presto, he's cured. By the Freudian process known as "transfer," he switches his own guilt to the analyst. He never needs another treatment and soon forgets all about his mother in the zestful effort to own a house again and perhaps a second pair of shoes.

The lesson is clear. When you can't afford to be sick, you stay well. Put illness within reach of everyone and we'll have a nation of invalids.

We tamper with Nature at our peril.

PRESCRIPTION

However clear this fundamental rule of healing is to us, we must admit that the general public does not understand it and the members of Congress understand it least of all. It must therefore be our constant concern to get the point across. I have nothing but commendation for those doctors who, for the last several years, have been prefacing each consultation with little sermonettes on socialized medicine and the sanctity of the patient-doctor relationship. Medical research has shown these to be extraordinarily effective when given as anaesthesia is taking hold just before a major operation.

It is vital, of course, to keep up your payments to the emergency fund in Washington. We have for long had the largest lobby in town, but we must increase our staff and increase our efforts. The population explosion and the creation of new states of the union have been sending new members of Congress to the capital yearly. Our people must meet them all, carry their bags, get them a cab, and in general show them that doctors are their friends. Naturally, this takes financial support; I can assure you that there is no better investment and, like most of you, I'm something of an expert in the investment field.

Some imaginative freedom fighters have combined these two techniques. Heavy givers to the emergency fund, they have prorated their donations among their patients and explained, by a sticker on the statement, that the surcharge will cease when the socializing threat ceases. The sticker also has room for the name of the congressman to write to. For anyone wishing to join the effort, a stack of statement-stickers will be found, appropriately, in the lobby.

But whether, as an individual practitioner, you adopt these new medical techniques or just continue in the invaluable, day-in, day-out campaign of doubling all fees when groups are involved, I urge eternal vigilance and renewed dedication to the professional ideal expressed in the chorus of the *Hymn to Hippocrates:*

Don't let them take it away.

*Don't let them
take it away*

Osborn

XVII
SOFT DEMONS IN HARD TIMES

NOTE:

THE ONLY unsolicited sample. One of the researchers, on a field trip in New York City, spent his weekends wandering about the streets with his pocket recorder turned on. Working under a creative fellowship from another foundation, he was gathering material for a new tape symphony of the city. There hadn't been one that semester. Late on Saturday afternoon in November, he passed an idle hour waiting for a crosstown bus outside the walls of the New Conservatives' Club. Apparently the highly sensitive microphone picked up a voice from the inside. At any rate, that night, when he began composing with scissors and adhesive, he discovered the following unpremeditated sample. As scholarly readers can imagine, this posed a pretty problem of equity between our foundation and the Foundation for Creative Musicology.

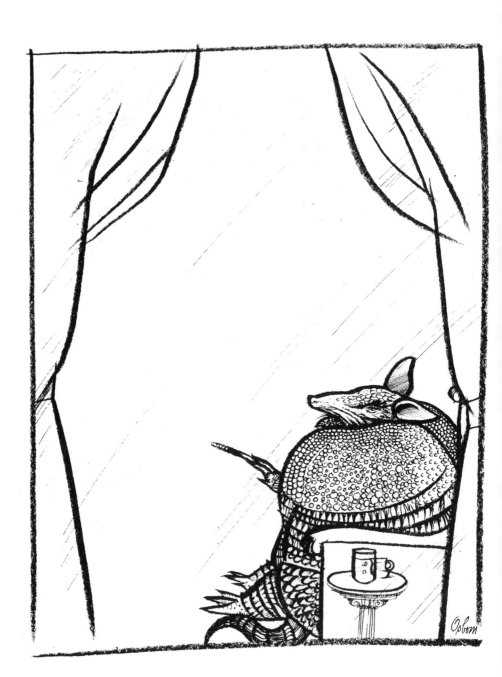

XVII
SOFT DEMONS IN HARD TIMES

HE DEMON of softness has been gnawing at America's vitals for a full generation now and we are gone soft not only in our vitals but in our muscles and bones, our brawn and brains, especially, perhaps, in our brains.

You can see it in the very food we eat. What the hell *is* cottage cheese, anyway? Does it have an independent, objective existence? Or is it a hallucination, a projection of our own affinity for the formless, the soft and squishy, the flesh without the bones. Speaking of bones, or speaking of without bones, look at the food the young mothers buy in the markets. That prepared baby food started it. When a mother mashed up peas and carrots for her child, something of her effort remained in the food and, while the fibers were broken down and all that, still there was character in the dish. Not so when you buy it all premashed in little jars. Did you know the harried mother can now buy mashed banana in those jars? It's the truth.

TWENTY DEGREES SOFTER ON THE INSIDE

Well, mother and child had such a jolly old time flinging mashed banana at each other, that the jolly old food monopolies soon made the fun available for all. It comes in a plate made of the foil they used to wrap cigarettes in and it's any flavor you want. The material—or the substance, I guess, is a better word—is the same stuff every time. It's made out of old bran mash shaped into assorted forms and covered with a thick veneer of bread crumbs. According to the market demand, these objects are packaged and labeled "shrimp," "steak," "veal," "scallops," "lamb," or what you will. The customer pops them into the oven—nobody ever just *puts* these things in an oven—serves them piping hot, and provides the only taste the stuff has with ketchup, sea-food sauce, sauce tartare, or mint-flavor jelly. A drop of honest Worcestershire would vaporize the lot. It gives you the illusion of having eaten with none of the hard work of chewing, swallowing, and digesting. It leaves the mind free to follow the similarly manufactured entertainment on television, and if you want to talk about softness we could go on for several days about that end of the Liederkranz.

Or take the chairs you sit and watch the color tapioca from. I have no brief for horsehair sofas, but by God when you sat on them you knew you were sitting on something. It kept you alert all the time. Well, then it was springs and strings and cushions. Then it was foam rubber, the all-purpose material for a soft civilization. Relax and roll over, you stupid bastard, you never had it so good, and they pick your pocket while you slumber. Not content with lolling around on lotus-land furniture made out of air, we have lately added massaging motors to that air and as you loll you get the excruciating pleasure of a hundred ethereal fingers stroking away the cares of the day. I tell you, sooner or later those chairs are going to be rounded up by the vice squad and there'll be a hell of a scandal.

BUT SOFT, WHAT BLIGHT

As I sit here, on this fine old horsehair sofa, in this splendid club, soon, no doubt, to be replaced by a parking lot for the sake of the increased turnover, as I sit, I say, glass in hand filled with properly aged and undiluted whiskey—and you know, in this as in so many things, Roosevelt didn't know what he was talking about when he denounced the bourbons of America; that crowd all drank Scotch—as I sit, back erect, eyes aglow, every fiber alert and alive, as I sit in this twilight of humanity, I ask myself, where did it all begin? How did this permeating softness creep into the national scene: How can we tolerate it so blithely? What will be the end of it all?

And I make my answer.

We went soft, it seems to me, during the Great Depression. They were rough years, make no mistake about it. I used to sit here in the club window and watch my former colleagues take the plunge from their neighboring offices into that flat splat where all accounts are balanced and the Great Receiver reckons up the assets and the liabilities.

But America had had hard times before that. We'd had panics so bad we gave up using the very word and I note, in passing, that "depression" has suffered the same fate: we have "recessions" and rolling readjustments; one of these days one of those readjustments is going to roll us right out the door. My point is that in the worst of the panics, we didn't really panic, but in the depression we allowed ourselves the luxury of feeling very depressed.

Well, that was softness right there, but then we institutionalized the softness. In the first place, the government assumed the responsibility of seeing that everyone had enough to eat. This is simply not a proper function of government. In the first place, you destroy initiative and incentive. It's all very well to talk about the second car and color television, but I tell you nothing activates a man more than not knowing where his next meal is coming from. If he has several children who are also hungry, so much the better.

SOFTLY, AS IN A-BORNING QUICKSAND

Doles and leaf-raking and government soup kitchens were bad enough, but then came Social Security, and this utterly dissolved any glint of hardness that may have survived the NRA. At a stroke this demonic device wiped out the traditional American desire to save for one's old age. The motive of that saving was basically to be able to look at one's contemporaries still working and congratulate oneself on one's thrift and industry. Now everyone retires and there's no incentive to virtue. Contraception, I may point out, did the same thing to virginity.

Speaking of virtues, Social Security has had a devastating effect on religion. One of the traditional sources of strength for our churches was the old folks' coming around for a handout and staying to learn about God. Social Security has destroyed this ancient relationship. The old folks get their groceries at the supermarket the same as the young folks, and if they maintain their ties to organized religion at all, those ties most often center on the weekly bingo games and the seasonal bazaars. I know that radical thinkers dismiss the traditional Christmas-basket approach as that of rice-Christians, but surely rice-Christians are preferable to dice-Christians.

Social Security was followed quickly by rampant unionism, in

a powerful movement that will not be satisfied until *all* industry, not just textiles, is located in the South, where they manage these things differently.

Unionism has totally enslaved the workingmen of America, who find themselves no longer free to negotiate with their employers over working conditions and wages, but forced to accept what the union decrees for all workers, good, bad, or indifferent. In hard times in the old days, the farsighted worker, by prudent domestic management, cutting down expenses, taking in his belt, and doing without the frills of life, was able to ensure himself of steady employment by simply offering to work for less than his competitors in the labor market. Now there is no true labor market at all. Certainly there's no competitive bidding, and the prudent worker is forced to abide by the standards set by the imprudent.

SOFT IN THE STILLY NIGHT

What is far more dangerous, however, is the effect these things —unionism, Social Security, and the graduated income tax—have had on the better classes of America. They just won't work any more, and who can blame them? Hedged in by restrictive laws on every side, badgered by power-mad union officials, and severely penalized for financial success, the fledgling captain of industry quite understandably says, The hell with it, and goes in for chorus girls, French impressionism or philanthropy.

Worse yet is the course taken more recently by the heirs of some of the outstanding industrial and financial heroes of the past, men like Harriman, Rockefeller, and Kennedy. The younger generation, despairing of ever making a dollar and hanging on to more than a dime of it, has given up completely. They've joined the enemy. They've gone into government.

With industry thus deprived of its natural leadership you get the top taken over by professional managers who haven't the vaguest idea of what they're supposed to be doing. What they're supposed to be doing is making profits for the shareholders, and all these managerial revolutionists can talk about is industrial statesmanship, service to the public, and inflated retirement plans for themselves. You put this kind of management together with unionized, overpaid labor and you get precooked dinners made of sawdust and chairs that commit mechanized indecent assault on you.

Happily the picture isn't all soft. I know you young fellows who live in the country take a different view of the New Haven railroad from that held by those of us who live safely in town, but try to put aside your personal feelings for a moment. The New Haven some years ago found that it could make more money as a bar and grill than in the transportation business. Fearlessly it made the correct management decision, and I ask you to remember this: every time you curse the train for being late, the line is reaping the harvest on perhaps a thousand extra martinis and thus, week by week, hour by hour even, staves off inevitable bankruptcy.

In *my* timetable, that's damn' smart railroading.

THE HARD FACTS

Scattered about the country, rather like Mr. Goldwater's hidden conservative majority, often, indeed, occupying the same space, are thousands of little pockets of resistance to the spreading softness. It is those hard pockets that give us courage. Because, sooner or later and it looks sooner all the time, the soft-soapers, soft-sellers, and soft-headed are going to get their way completely. When they do, the economic, political, and social structure of this country is going to melt into a little pool of nothing and run softly down the nearest drain.

When that happens the whole country, even the unionizers and the Social Securityizers, will turn for help to the only source available. They will beg the better classes, the hard men of old, the men who really know how, to take hold of things and put the country back in business. Naturally, we will assent to this only on our own terms, for only on those terms can the thing be done at all.

And then
we'll
see.

And then we'll see

Osborn

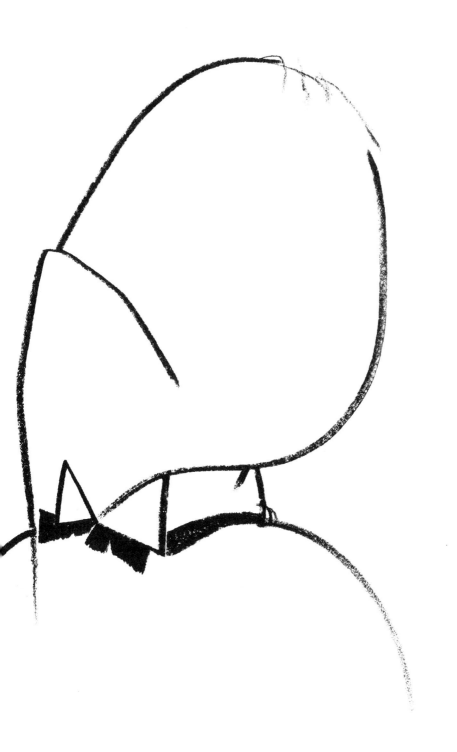

XVIII
THE DEMONS IN DEPTH

NOTE:

THE FOLLOWING is the transcript of a taped interview between the director of demonology and the director of the Institute for Para-Socio-Psychology in the Middle West. The institute director was unaware of the precise occupation of the demonological director. Their meeting took place at the annual convention of directors of the learned disciplines. To the director of demonology, the evidence of the director of the institute seemed peculiarly apropos since it was from just such directions that the strongest opposition to demonology once came.

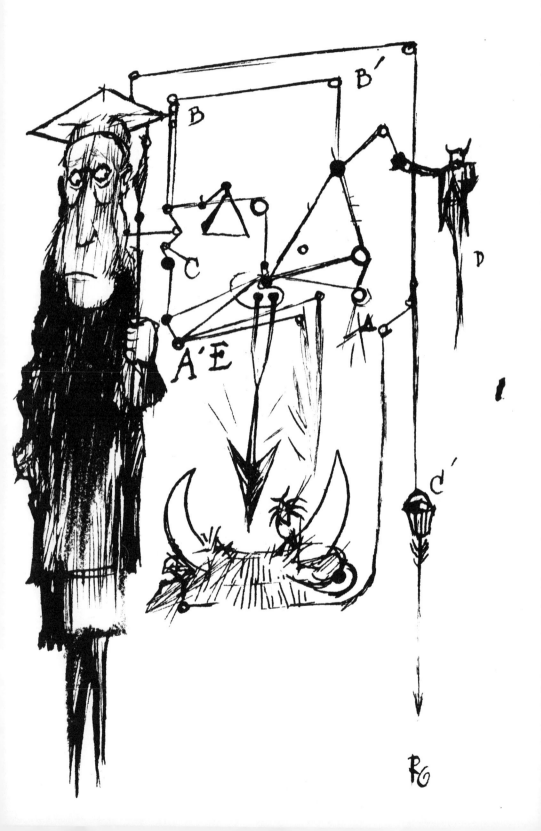

XVIII
THE DEMONS IN DEPTH

$\mathfrak{A}$ T ONE time it was thought that the affairs of the world really were influenced, if not actually managed, by demons. These demons were taken to be intelligent but not corporeal creatures, at least not corporeal in the sense that mankind is. The demons were thought to have their origin variously as God-created angels who had chosen to rebel or as the "other half" of the spirit world, the spirits turned toward darkness in a universe balanced on equal opposition between light and dark, good and evil. The demons had as the ends of such actions of theirs as impinged upon the human continuum the corruption and ruin of human beings and the general bad-going of the world. The demons took as their means for these ends everything from tormenting mankind with plagues and earthquakes to the actual spiritual occupation of individual men, who, having lost their own will to that of the demon, were said to be "possessed."

COMPARATIVE CASE HISTORIES FROM THE PHYSICAL SCIENCES

The latter history of the demons, as of demonism and demonology, is well enough known to require but the slightest of references here. Ignorant man—and mark that the qualification is "ignorant," and not either "stupid" or "ill-willed"—ignorant, then, man knew for ages that if, for example, he stepped off the edge of a precipice he would most probably fall very rapidly to the bottom, where, depending on the height of the fall, his own position upon re-establishing contact with the earth, the nature of the surface at the bottom, and other variables, he would find himself in one of several stages of serious misfortune. (Normally, these range from bruises and lacerations through partial dismemberment to total misfortune, or "death.")

Now, as we have since scientifically verified, ignorant man's belief that this chain of events would follow his stepping off the cliff was essentially correct. Ignorant, but prudent, man therefore took it as a rule of conduct not to step off cliffs. Ignorant man, however, attributed the chain of events subsequent to stepping off cliffs to the wrong reasons; he attributed it to demons, who, he imagined, were able to get at him in the air more easily than on solid ground, and who, in his naive world-view, abruptly seized him by the legs and yanked him down into the abyss.

Thus, when ignorant man avoided the edges of cliffs and especially avoided stepping off such edges, we may say that he performed a correct action for the wrong reasons.

Presently the physical scientist Newton made his studies and came up with some new answers. In the post-Newtonian world-view, man, no longer ignorant, has learned that if he steps off the precipice he will, as before, fall directly to the bottom and will, at the very least, be bruised and, at most, be killed, but he now knows that this is due, not to demons, but to gravity. When, therefore, well-informed man nowadays avoids the edges of cliffs, we may say that this is a good action for the right reason. The change, although slight in outward conduct, is a significant advance in mankind's slow climb toward consciousness and rationality.

COMPARATIVE CASE HISTORIES FROM THE PARA-SOCIO-PSYCHOLOGICAL SCIENCES

Much the same process of new information shedding light on old problems, behavior patterns, and observable phenomena has, of course, been taking place in the non-physical sciences. For example, ignorant man, when he had successfully avoided the edge of the cliff and got home to the village once more, might find that the man up the street had filled his day, not with the socially acceptable and personally advisable activity of avoiding the edges of cliffs, but with the unsocial action of chopping up his mother with a lumberman's ax.

In the olden times ignorant man and his fellow ignorant villagers would, it is presumed, attribute this action to the influence

of demons upon the woodsman. They would most likely kill the culprit on the grounds that he had taken a life and must therefore lose his own. Or they might conceivably judge his demonic infestation to be such as required isolating him from the community. They would therefore place him in some kind of confinement, perhaps for a given period of time but probably for the rest of his life in the curious belief that this would help prevent such occurrences in the future. In the light of reason we can see the folly of this course, for, after all, the man had but one mother and, having killed her, may be presumed to have worked out completely his suppressed tendencies toward matricide.

How differently, thanks to modern advances in the psychosocial sciences, we handle such things today.

Today, our judicial machinery is still based on the antiquated notions of "punishment" for "crime" and of what is called "the protection of society." As if society could be protected from primal human urges that lie buried deep in the unconscious of every man and that take study, experimentation, and patient, day-by-day labor on the part of para-psycho-social scientists to recognize, uncover, and cure. But in spite of that archaic legal system, we are still able to help society prevent the dreadful waste of a second human life just because one has already, unfortunately, been sacrificed. Today we see at once that the man who kills his mother has something wrong with him. He is sick. He is, in fact, a very sick man. But he can be cured. How much better it is, for society and for the man himself, to undertake the cure and, after a few

years—necessary not so much for the treatment as to give society a chance to forget—to return the patient to active life.

THE DEMONS ARE MARCHING HOME AGAIN, HURRAH

To those of us actually engaged in the slow process of remaking mankind and with him society, it seems self-evident that this is worth-while work. Yet there is opposition, constant opposition, ranging from vulgar heckling to vicious and sometimes successful legal suits. As the classic example and undoubtedly an extremely influential factor in the general lack of co-operation we encounter, I cite the sensation-mongering attitude of the American press. In a case like the one just hypothesized, for example, the press would, from the very beginning, have made rational judgment impossible for most laymen—a term that here, of course, includes members of the bar and of the bench—by printing all available details on the unfortunate event itself and on the full background of the patient. Worse still, assuming that the patient's treatment was successful and he was released, the press could be counted upon to dredge up the whole sorry business all over again, thus inevitably starting the patient's postconvalescence on a very bad note.

Under the circumstances it is hardly surprising that such a patient occasionally suffers a relapse, with a complete repetition of his original symptomatic action, namely, the doing away with another human being. Then it is that the press shows its true colors and invariably takes the side of obscurantism against progress. Both events are reviewed thoroughly, with all available photographs. Statements by responsible psychiatrists are held up to ridicule and the press leads public opinion in any orgy of denunciation of all the latest thought in both para-socio-psychology and para-psycho-sociology.

I suppose I need not lecture you on the timidity of politicians. At moments like these they seem to lose all their faith in science. They issue rash statements and they pass rash laws. Some very good men have lost important penological consulting posts in such circumstances. Worse still, the patient in question, who, now if ever, is ready for a complete cure, is taken out of our hands and permanently put away, in one way or the other.

Hence my growing belief, scarcely as yet formulated into a hypothesis, that we may have been hasty in putting down the demons. They may, after all, be still alive, still prowling the edges of our world, seeking whom they may devour, corrupting the press, intimidating governments, and turning every man's hand against true science.

COMPLIANCE WITH SCIENCE

What would be more natural, when you think about it, than for the demons—decisively defeated and deprived of domain by the para-sciences—to bide their time and now strike back disguised as tabloid editors, as indignant letter writers, and as wee, sleekit, cowrin', tim'rous governors and members of parole boards?

Doctors are always discovering that the old discredited folk-remedies have a scientific basis after all. One of the major branches of contemporary literature is devoted to such rediscoveries. Something similar may be going on with the demons.

If so, the time is ripe for demonological rediscovery, reunmasking and repurging of our society. Was the Inquisition really a mistake? Can't we put a torque in Torquemada?

THE CLIENTS FOR SCIENCE

For the truth is, we in the para-sciences are on the very threshold of reshaping the world. The stakes are too high to allow a handful of demons, relicts from a cruder age and motivated out of sheer spite, to wreck the dream we can build. All our activities with penitentiary patients point to the remaking of human nature. Again, back at the institute, through drugs and the weaving of baskets, we have been able to calm down and redirect the most furious energies. But in every case, however obvious our success, we are faced with the same problem: sooner or later the patient leaves the institute and returns to the outside world and to the problems that sent him to us in the first place. Months of scientific endeavor vanish in a moment.

What we need is to control the outside world, too. And it can be done. The demons confine themselves mainly to the sphere of politics. Unknown to them, we have outflanked them. Our agents are entrenched in business and industry, in education, in medicine, in vast areas of communications. For merchandising, for music and drama on the tiny screen, for wit and wisdom at the fireside, people consult us as they once did fortunetellers. Surely this is power as valid and as potent as that of elected officials. Surely this is the key to placid living for everyone and to universal destiny guided and controlled by the people equipped to do it, the para-psycho-socio-scientists of the new age.

ALLIANCE WITH SCIENCE

As with the patients in penitentiaries and as with patients at the institute itself, the means already exist. The problem is solely one of their application. That in turn resolves itself largely into the problem of dealing with the demons in press and politics. Both fields are notoriously corrupt; yet both, beyond readership surveys and private polls on the para-psycho-socio aspects of new policies and personalities, remain strangely deaf to the logic of science. Both have a fixation on what they call civil rights, a set of archaic "protections" of the individual against society. The point they miss is that such legal safeguards were necessary and desirable in earlier ages, if for nothing else to permit the rise of the para-sciences. The old-time policeman, like the old-time landlord, had to be limited in his power because his goals were selfish and his ignorance appalling. Para-science desires only the good of society and of the individuals who compose it. Para-science also has the knowledge to bring these goods about. In such a situation, such a concept as civil rights becomes, not only superfluous, but a positive detriment to human progress.

It may well be that a new demonology is the answer. It may well be that the demons have survived their destruction and are with us still, standing between mankind and his noblest vision.

It may well be that the obstacle can be removed.

EVALUATION

VALUATION IS extremely difficult, especially meaningful evaluation. The foregoing samples are all rather raw, some, of course, more so than others. Could Columbus, one asks, seeing the gulls two days off San Salvador, possibly have envisioned the busses on Madison Avenue or the looping freeways of Los Angeles? If he had, wouldn't he have cut about and hoisted full sail for Spain? Could Socrates, strolling through Athens with his fellow-idlers, have caught the faintest glimmer of the Yale Bowl and the higher studies in hotel management? If so, wouldn't he, for all the heroics with the hemlock, have stopped asking people those silly questions?

So it is through history. Evaluation is difficult. Special circumstances, one in particular, render the necessary task even more troublesome in concluding the present study. Yet the task must be attempted; certain tentative conclusions must be, if not drawn, at least indicated. For one thing, it's expected.

We may say, then, that the evidence seems to point to the following working hypotheses:

1. Far from having vanished with the dawn of enlightenment, the demons merely took other forms and are very clearly working today as they always did.

2. All the data, raw as it is, indicates a new level of perception on the part of those engaged in finding demons, in describing their dominant characteristics, and in taking steps to thwart demonic activity.

3. Yet this heightened perception and the action that flows from it are still scattered, disorganized, and inefficient. A factor

231

prolonging this condition is the pluralistic nature of American society. Depending on where the individual observer is stationed within that society, he may see an entirely different set of demons from that seen from another station.

4. This indicates that a revival of the ancient discipline of demonology is certainly overdue—just as we suspected before we began running the tests.

5. But demonology today—both theoretical and practical—will almost certainly take new forms, probably unrecognizable by the practitioners of classical demonology in the golden age of the seventeenth century. For whereas a really competent demonologist then was in one sense the agent of his entire society, and in another the guiding spirit of that society, this can no longer be true. The new demonologist will almost certainly resemble a broker between interested and competing parties rather than an agent or guide of any one of them.

6. The final conclusion also is one that we suspected strongly at the outset, but that now has a sizable body of scientific evidence to back it up: New funds must be sought.

Inquiries are invited.

NOTE:

THE ABRUPT introduction of an "Evaluation" at this
point was necessitated by the following circumstance. Shortly after his return from the isle of Capri,
the director was asked to come to the offices of the foundation,
housed, as it happens, in those of the firm that is the principal
donor. There it was explained to him that the firm had been
having a bad year and that only a certain percentage of its
income was deductible as educational, scientific, and cultural
encouragement, a percentage that had been reached during
his side trip to Paris. Funds were therefore cut off until the
profit situation and the tax situation made them again available. Since it was hinted rather broadly that such availability
may be far in the future, the director, in his decision-making
role, gave the order to publish at once.

INDEX